DEDICATION UNTO MY KIDS

BY

MICHELLE JEAN

This book is dedicated to my children. All of you have taught me so much in life.

You've taught me that you can rise above adversity no matter the circumstances, no matter the trials and tribulations.

In all I have been through in life you were all right there with me.

God you are not excluded from this because you were right there holding my hand though the storms and tsunami's. You are a part of my family and yes you are my baby and you will forever be my true love.

To you all I dedicate this book and hope you find true love and favor in all the words.

To God and my Children thank you all for being apart of my life and I love you all unconditionally.

Mommy/Michelle

God help me to open the eyes of my children and make them understand and overstand that in life we have to think of others. You have to live for life and not death.

Help me to let them know and see that they must do good unto others despite the wrongs others have done unto them

They need to know that the race is on in life and giving out of **true love** beats all because anyone can say they love but not everyone or anyone can say they truly love

Thinking of the poor and less fortunate beats all and giving to give means nothing at all. Truly love to give not give to get

Do not give to accumulate wealth because all you do will be taken from you meaning you die and will never fully enjoy life nor will you fully enjoy your wealth

Never measure wealth in materialistic gain because material possessions are left behind but spiritual wealth is life eternal

A rich man can have all the material possessions today but tomorrow he can lose it all because of greed

No I am not rich financially and a lot of times I come crying to you God for financial help, emotional help, spiritual help and guidance. This I do best because I know you as well as know the relationship I have in you and with you.

God the little I do I am hoping will help you, my children and all those that will now come to you and follow you in truth and honesty.

It's not all about me
It's about you
You're helping me to help others
Whether it be family or strangers

God open the eyes of my children
Let them see this
Let them know this
Let them see the needs of others
Not just the needs of themselves
Let them extend a helping hand to those that truly need you

God let them come and do greater goodness in you than I have done. Let them truly know you and your goodness and with this goodness let them cleave to it and never let it you. And God for the record they must never let go of you because you are true and good to me and them.

Michelle

God it hurts me to hear how my son talks
It hurts me to hear him say he doesn't
care if he dies

Yes we have come along way
They have seen things young children
should not have to see. Trials and
tribulations that children should not have
to go through and trust me they have been
through it all.

They have scars
Scars that will take a long time to heal if
they heal at all

God they have done nothing wrong and at
times I blame myself for the choices I've
made in my life

I know my son is hurt
But he needs to see the hurt of others and
not just his hurt

Yes we are disappointed in life
Others disappoint you
But he has to learn at times it's not about
him, others have things to do

It is hard because I have been
disappointed in life by others but I have
learnt to accept these disappointments
and move on. I have learned to rely on you
with every aspect of my life. God with you
I can tell you everything and I do tell you
everything. Sometimes I even say God you

pick the panties and clothes that you want me to wear today. I even tell you you have to take me lingerie shopping or I need you to buy me this dress. To people this may sound weird or crazy but with me and you this isn't crazy because I know in time we will go shopping just me and you but right now it has to do with money – my financial setbacks. But I am not financially set back because I am paying my bills in a timely fashion and soon all my financial debts the debts I have accumulated will be all be paid in full because I know my sinful debts are paid in full and I owe the devil and his people nothing.

It wasn't easy for you because I came with a lot of problems. Problems that I am just overcoming and it wasn't man that made me overcome them it was you. God no one can take my true love from you because I know and those who know me truly know what you have brought me through.

As for disappoints I am learning they can work in my favour and bring me joy and sometimes they do.

God I hope my children not just my son learn these things and make positive changes in his life – their lives. He is a good kid a young man of values with a good heart.

Michelle

My children hear me now and in everything that you do do it honestly
Be honest about life
Be honest in life
Be faithful and true to God
Be truthful to yourself
Be truthful to God

My children it's not everyone that say they are with you are with you this is why I tell you to know who your true friends are.

If you cannot find a true friend in man find a true friend in God. Make God your true friend above any man or anything because when man and beast yes even spirit fail you God cannot and will never fail you.

Know that humanity is jealous and yes God is jealous too so know your friends because some of them are your enemies and you will not know it. They are that cunning and deceitful. Rely on God to show you them and this God will do using trees, nuts and colours as in the colours of the rainbow so know the colours of God and how it is being used.

Remember some of your friends will set you up and cause you to fall due to jealousy and greed so follow your spirit and know what your spirit is saying to you.

Some will do things to make you fall
A lot will hurt you dearly – badly but leave them to God and never ever infinitely never ever lift a finger to hurt them. Always remember what no ketch quakoo must catch shirt. Meaning if sorrow do not catch the person that is inflicting sorrow and pain it will one day catch his or her children.

Find it in your hearts to forgive them meaning find it in your hearts to forgive your enemy because the good and the bad must call upon God no matter if it is in the end of their life – on their death bed.

Always remember that a good man or woman worries not about his soul/spirit but evil worries about it all the time. He or she is consumed about it even kill thinking that they can maintain and sustain it.

Always remember evil kills and does kill but good cannot kill because good lives in truth at all times. Good is life but evil is death.

In all that people do to you to hurt you never lift a finger to harm them - hurt them

Always always always pray by talking to God and making him know your feelings – darkest thoughts and the way to pray is through silent thought. Remember when all is gathered at the table the father say prayer or grace. If he elects a child to say grace – prayer the prayer must be for the family and it must be good and appropriate. If there is no father the mother is the elected head of the table and she too can elect a child to grace – pray for the family by giving thanks to God. If mother and father is not around then the eldest must take the reign or the place of the parent. If the eldest is a female she is the head of the household. If the eldest is a male then he is the head of the household. He or She must teach right and pray right they cannot be false in their teachings.

Also remember your mind will urge you to do harm but do not listen to your mind. It will deceive you and cause you to fall.

Always do good no matter how senseless it may seem in your eyes

My children I am not a good teacher this is why I write these things to you all. This is my way to communicate with you all.

My children hear me I beg of you

Listen to me and my words

Never turn from God
Walk in his integrity

Walk in his true love

Let him lead you and do good always

All that you do

Do out of true love and do it for God

Store up everything in God
Love, friends, your home, family
Everything good deed that you do store it up in God. If you have a universe full of money store it up in God and tell him to use a portion of it to help those that re in need. I know you are saying how can I store up my money in God he is not a bank. No he's not a bank but the same principle applies but instead of leaving all in the bank you are telling God to use a portion of your money to help someone – others. It's hard to explain but I hope in time God will open your eyes and let you comprehend what I am saying to you. This too is your blessing. God knows what to do. Think of the money as your blessing you have an abundance of it so do not keep it for yourself trust God to use this blessing wisely and in a positive way. Tell him to use to do good and never use it to do evil because God is both good and evil. Remember he is ALL – Allelujah.

Every goodness that you do store it up in God and never ever do anything for greed. When you do out of greed you will live to regret it because one act of kindness wipes away numerous sins.

Mom

Father God in all thy goodness I beg thee mercy and goodness for my children

Father, in all thy love your true love I beg you forgiveness for my children

Father, please open their eyes to true love – the truth
Open their eyes to the needs of others
Open their eyes to the evils of this world. Let them see it but never ever infinitely never ever let men walk in evil nor bask in evil. Let them stay away from evil and walk in your goodness as well as their goodness only. God all that I ask I ask out of truth and true love for you. Do not meaning never disappointment me. God I many not have asked you this before they were born but I am asking you now. Now that I know the truth I am asking you truthfully because I know with you we can never be too late for a shower of rain meaning your goodness.

My children many will forsake you
God many will forsake them

Many will want to use them

Many will play tricks on them
But I know you will stand by them against
the enemy. You will protect them and keep
them safe.

Father it is not easy on my children
Please open their eyes to you and your
goodness yes your true love.

Father, show them
Teach them that people will fail them
Tell lies on them
Persecute them
But you will never fail them

Father, show them all these things
Show them to have total faith, love and
trust in you

Father, do not disappoint me
Please do not fail me

Father I truly love them
Want and need what's best for them but I
cannot do this alone

I truly need you

Father, great is my love for you
Great is my love for them

Father, please educate them truthfully
and honestly as you have educated me

Father, they are my life because you are my friend and love they are my friend and love too

Father great is my love for them too that is why I am coming to you and asking you for mercy in raising them, educating them in all that is true ad good in you.

Father, truly love them, protect them and keep them safe from harm

Father, you gave me them but I am just a woman with earthly teachings

Father, your teachings is perfect, better than mine. Therefore, I leave them in your good care

Your loving arms

Michelle

My children you are my love
My life
Great is my love for thee

There are many things I cannot teach you
Yes at times I will fail you but never for
one moment think that I don't truly love
all of you

My children, four are you
Four that is precious in my sight

Four different spirits

We've had many rough times
Many bad times
Yes we had a lot of ups and downs
Many failures too
But never for one moment think that I
don't truly love you

All four of you are my hope for a better
future, a better and brighter tomorrow.

May God eternally bless all of you
May he shower you all with his love, grace,
mercy and blessings

My children, all my love
I love you all unconditionally

Mom

My children

My kids never give to get something in return

Do all the goodness that you can do from the true love of thy heart

Do goodness in the name of God

My children – kids hear my words
Cleave to them
Do right by them

Although I am poor
I am rich in love – true love and I am loved by God

Do not look upon our surroundings
Material possessions mean nothing in the sight of God

Love
True love is a whole different thing
Remember anyone can say I love you
But not many can truly love
Truly say I truly love you

True love is honest
Truthful
Patient
It does not hurt

True love can never be blind but love is blind because love is based on death –

vanity. People love for different reasons and at the end of the day love turn into evil. What you can get out of the other person. How much pain you can inflict when it comes to the next person even your kids because they too get caught in the crossfire of humanities love games yes humanities lying game.

True love is not blind to the follies of the world

It is not blind to the follies of the heart

My children when you truly love you will want to do no wrong

My children when you truly love you have the true love of God

You walk in the true love and integrity of God

My children it's not to say people will not hurt you, they will hurt you

Some will not understand you
Some will confuse you
Try to kill you

My children do not walk blindly in the world and do not walk in the way of evil. Remember Psalms 1 blessed is the man that walketh not in the council or the ungodly nor sitteth at the seat of the scornful. For his delight is in the laws of the Lord for which he meditate day and night.

See it and know the evils of this world

Know the evil people that reside with you in this world and stay away from them. Separate yourself from evil. This was how it was in the beginning and this is the way it must be in the end.

My children there are many evil people out there. They say they are with you. They will stand with you. Many come as beautiful angels. Angels of light, angels of God but they are deceivers. They walk and commission the death. Use the dead to do their dirty deeds. Use the dead to try and kill you. Do not worry about them but call on God at all times. God is the only one that can number them as well as count and measure their evil deeds. Always remember when God protects and shield you evil must go back to sender.

Do not think for one minute that these people will not hurt you. They will hurt you. They will find some excuse to hurt you to justify their wrongs. Never forget evil kills and it must take a life. This is how evil is maintained and sustained upon this planet. Evil must kill all good people and when they do evil will turn on its own because evil is faithful to no one.

The job of evil is evil and evil is not partial nor does evil play favorites. Evil lives for death whether the person is good or bad. All must die in evil's eye.

Everything hath life but it is not everything that lives always remember that. Yes the air that we breathe hath life it is that which sustains and maintains us. The water that we drink hath life because it also sustains and maintains us. Yes the dark hole hath life because the darkness that you see houses and contains life. Man cannot see this because man knows not of this. Let no one tell you there is no life in that darkness because there is life. Remember I told you everything hath life including evil but it is not everyone or everything lives. Some die and this is by choice meaning evil choose and chose to kill life.

And do not say Ma the air did not chose. No it did not but evil chose for it meaning evil kills it by polluting it. Man cannot kill the air we breathe nor can they kill the water we drink because man cannot kill the universe and that which governs it. Evil cannot do it either because the universe belongs not to evil and man but it belongs to God and the goodness of God.

Evil will try to break you
But don't give in no matter the tears and fears. Know this to be infinitely true if you

do not let evil into your abode and life evil cannot come in. In order for you to let evil in it must be invited in. Evil cannot go where it is not invited. Remember it only takes one invitation and it does not have to be from you. It can be from your wife or children so teach your family well. Once evil is invited in it will keep coming back because he has an all access pass to your life and your abode. Nothing that you do will get evil out. This is where God comes in you have to rely on God to set you and your family free.

Know that evil hath no shame or disgrace because evil has no morals. It hath not the truth of Love. Evil is not true it is a lie and it does lie. Trust me his lies will seem like the truth and this is why I tell you and will forever tell everyone know God and not just believe in God. You must know because when you know evil can never ever infinitely never ever deceive you. If you do not know trust me God will show you the truth and when he does listen. Do you hear me listen to God. And no God would infinitely never ever tell you to rape rob and steal. God would infinitely never ever tell you to kill anyone because God is life and life cannot kill.

No matter how much you weep

Lift up your cries always to God and he will deliver you. God will take you perfectly away from evil doers.

If you feel evil is doing you harm meaning if you feel the touch of evil in anyway pray to God. You may not know the person that is using evil against you meaning the person that has went to the voodoo priest or shaman, obeah man you name it. Pray to God truthfully. If you are not doing anything to the person and you are not in their way tell God by saying God I do not know what is happening but I am not standing in evils way but yet evil is hurting me. God this is not fair to me because I am not doing anything to them I am living my life as well as I am trying to live by your truth and integrity. God lift the hands of evil from around me and my family shield us if it's you alone say shield me, protect me from evil and return evil back to sender. God what right does evil have to hurt me when I am not interfering with evil and evil people. God my hands are clean of evil so why should they hurt me when I have done them nothing. God look at me and deal fair and just with me in thy sight and truly save me. Pray in this manner and God will see you through but remember you have to be clean. Meaning you cannot be harming people and pray in this manner because God will turn from you because you are not truthful and honest. You too are doing evil in the sight of God.

Some people will tell you use the Psalms or use this Psalms with water or this candle or with parchment paper do not listen to them. Run dem. When dem sey use oil a diss and oil a dat RUN DEM do you hear me. Run dem because with God there is no use or need for these evil things. God don't use oil or parchment paper when he is blessing you. He does you use water meaning if you ask him to shower down his blessing on you he will shower you with water meaning let it rain on you in your vision or dreams.

Yes it also means you must not use water to harm anyone because God does not use it to harm you.

Mom

My children people will come and go in your lives

Many will say they are your friends but behind your back they deceive you

Some will offer you a pot of Gold

Some will tell you everything is okay

Know them because they are not with you

Never put your trust in man because man will fail you

Put your trust in God he will never fail you. He will hide you, protect you

We are flesh but no matter the flesh the flesh cannot fail you. The flesh will never fail you, all it can do at the end of its allotted lifetime is decay. Return unto the dust of the earth when the soul has completed its task here on earth

Let no man tell you that the flesh is weak because the flesh means nothing. It replenishes the earth through the aide of worms that eat it.

Hear me my children and cleave onto my words and let my words educate you.

The mind – yes the mind is a powerful tool and weapon. It is strong and it does fail.

Your mind will paint a perfect picture

Make fools gold look real

It will and can take white gold and turn it into silver

My children be careful of the mind because it can and will deceive you then turn and laugh at you

The mind will tell you to cheat
Tell you to do all that is bad
It will tell you to leave your wife for facial beauty
It will cause you to lust
It will cause you to give up your earthly and spiritual possessions
Cause you to walk away from your kids
Cause you to walk and seek after greed
Cause you to walk after unlawful things
Commit unlawful acts

My children the flesh is nothing but flesh, but the mind will cause you to turn from God. This is the goal of the mind. Its goal is to turn you from God. From living the way God wants you to live.

The mind is very strong and powerful because it lives in both the physical and spiritual. The mind knows about God and when you are on the right path it will do whatever it will to keep you from God.

Know this. A prime example is when you are praying to God. Connecting to God it will drop a thought in the conversation just to throw you off.

My children always know the truth
Always know that God never kills. He is true love, he never hurts.

Yes, the mind hurts, even plays psychological games – tricks

It is very angry and dark

Yes, it can be loving, very loving, but it is cunning so beware of the mind as it can and will cause you to kill. It will deceive you so do not live for the mind. Try not to let it control you you control it.

My children, hear me, listen to me and be careful of the mind because it is very deadly. Trust me when you think you know it you don't so always be mindful and careful of the mind.

Mom

God thank you for my many blessings
Thank you for my kids

Thank you for protecting them
Thank you for watching over them

Father, although they don't listen at times
they are there for me

Yes they get on my nerves at times but I
get on there's too
Father God thank you for making me live
to see the true love in them

At times they are not mindful

At times they are influenced by friends but
God they are mine, they are yours too and
thank you for giving them to me

Father, the problems are real with them
and my hope and desire is that you teach
them honestly and truthfully so that they
can turn to you in honesty and truth.

Father God cleanse them
Take perfect hold of them and lead them
to your righteousness and truth. God
never let them go astray or follow the ways
of the wicked lest I be angry at you. As I
need you they too need you to hold their
hand and direct them in the right
direction.

Father, they will resist but I know you will take full charge of them. I know you will care for them and truly love them as you truly love me.

God I don't want or need any other God a part from you for them so please hear my plea and take charge of them and me.

Michelle

God please do not let my children go onto the way of the wicked.

Let them not walk in the way(s) of the wicked nor eat and drink in the pavilions of the wicked but let them walk in your footsteps, eat and drink in your home.

God whatever nets that are set for them, turn back the destruction and do not let it catch them or conquer them.

Whatever traps the enemy lay, do not let it ever befall my children or me

God I've come along way as well as know how evil and wicked people can be therefore I a pleading with you for my children, my family and the families you have given me

I am pleading with you for mercy, grace and favor for us all because it will not be an easy road.

God you know me as well as my thoughts. I do not want to see anyone on the face of this planet fall. I do not want my children nor do I need them to become the footstool for the enemy. You as well as I know how vile evil can be. You know how vile wicked people can be but this madness has to stop. Enough is enough God. You cannot continue to allow humanity be the stomping ground of the wicked.

I've shed many a tears for my country

I've shed many tears for my children and family I cannot let them fall. You cannot let them fall at the hands of the wicked. This is not just nor is it fair.

God please take hold of my family, my children and the families you have given to me. Secure them in your loving arms because I know soon blood will run like river upon the face of the earth if humanity do not shape up and start living for life.

Father God the mind is strong but you are stronger and safer.

You are the giver of life the creator of all and it is this all humanity calls out to no matter if we are good or bad.

God always let them (my children) see the nets and traps of the enemy before them at all times

Let them see the enemy too

God let no trouble befall them and in all you do let them turn to you, cherish you and truly love you

Have mercy upon them Father
Have mercy upon me.

Let them forever do good unto you, forever do good unto others

Father for thy mercies sake let them forever walk with you as well as cleave to you.

God you protect the good and the bad but yet evil seek to destroy all. Evil kills and reeks havoc on life and you cannot continue to allow this to happen anymore. We need life and not death. We need you today but we all have to clean up ourselves. God along the way we lost you but today I accept all of you – the goodness that you do.

Michelle

God I know it's not too late to turn my kids around

I know it's not too late to reach them

Father God take from my kids a deceitful and greedy heart

Take from them a covetous mind

Father, all that is evil in thy sight take it from them

From this day forth let them walk in your true love and integrity

Never let them fall from grace or become one of the wicked

God you are the perfect teacher so teach them the truth about life

Teach them the truth about you

You are the perfect father, mother, friend, comforter, confidant, everything

Father, the evils of this world is great
The evils unforgiving and abominable and I can say we are mere mortals but that is no excuse. If I said that I would be making excuses for humanity and that would be wrong. I am not here to make excuses but to ask you for your saving grace for my children and me

God as I ask you for mercy and love for them please find favour in them and help them to do all that is right and just in thy sight. God do not let them become like the children of old. Do not let them become stiff necked and haade ears. God as I need you they need you too.

God truly loving you is great

God do not turn from you because I am making this decision with you. God this is the right choice. Life is right and you are life so please do not disappoint me. God I need this for my children as well as their off springs. God none not one can or must walk in the way of evil for infinite generations.

God you told me you are with me and I can't walk without you I know this and I am trying to do right by you but you also have to do right by me and my family as well as the family you have given me. You cannot allow us nor can you let us be sacrificial lambs going to the slaughter house for evil. It is wrong. Evil stops now God. I am truly asking you for peace. I need you to truly squash this because I cannot see innocent lives die at the hands of evil anymore. What right does evil have to take innocent lives like that?

God I know we sin and I know about dirty and yes I know you have tried to save man and we are the ones to fail you turn from you but God look back truly look back and see the mistakes. God you know that evil ties people to him meaning evil binds us to it and once we are bound by evil we cannot get out of this bind. You know this God. I have seen it because you showed me this. It has happened to me. I was in hell and I lived in hell. I know the chains of hell and I have told you that not even my worst enemy I would wish this fate upon. I told you not even the Satan himself I want to go to hell but he made his choice.

God no one knows because they cannot see their future in hell. I know it because I've seen it and I have been there. You know it is not pretty but I cannot interfere with the Ying and the Yang to do this is to go against you and I cannot do this. It is wrong.

What evil is doing is wrong because he is causing humanity – life to die and no one has stood up to stop him. God evil can be stopped but we cannot do this alone we need you. We need you we truly need you and you know this. I know this and this is why I am pleading with you not just for myself, not just for my children and the families you have given me but for all of humanity including the animals. God I am pleading for life all life including the trees and water, the air that we breathe. God you are the breath of life please do not let evil and wicked people take our life. Do not let them take our hope from us anymore. God you are my hope our hope please do not let evil continue to take you away from us. It's not right nor is it fair to us but yet you let evil continue to do this. You cannot say you truly love us and continue to let evil slaughter us like pigs. Many things we did not know. You can break this tie please break it. You cannot let evil continue to rob us of our God given rights. This is wrong and you know it.

Good cannot go against evil you know this but evil has no right to go against life. Evil constantly break the rules so let evil suffer. Why should good people die amongst evil or go down with evil. We did not choose evil God we chose life I chose life for me and my children as well as the families you have given me. I am choosing that which is right and just for them therefore I am choosing honesty, peace, prosperity, true love, life and all the goodness and beauty that is you for them. God this is our bond for infinite generations. This bond cannot be broken by man or spirit and it cannot be broken by me or you no matter the fights I have with you because you don't fight nor do you argue with me. God You gave me seeds and I am choosing good seeds that will yield good plants as well as good fruits. Fruits that are grounded and rooted in your goodness – You and truly infinitely truly love you as I love you if not more.

You more than deserve our love – our true love.

Yes I know we have strayed from you so many times before but you still held us down. You still showed us true love because it is a truly loving being and person that leaves the sun and moon to shine on the good and the bad at the same time. You did not take the sun, moon and stars from us. You left them to keep us warm, cool us down

Father, what are we without you?

What are we without your true love?

Father, please take care of my children for my sake but more importantly for thy mercies sake.

MJ

Father God forsake me not

Forsake not my children but teach them to do good by you as well as cleave to you

Father, turn them from their wrongful ways, the ills of the heart, the ills of the people of this world.

Father, let all four of them come to truly love each other, rely on each other but more importantly rely on you

Father, let all four of them always be there for each other.

Let them not forsake each other, cheat nor deceive each other

Let them always admit when they are wrong

Always admit to their wrongs

Teach them your laws father

Teach them your laws and let them truly cleave to you.

Michelle

My children it is not all I can teach you because I do not know it all. There will come a point in time when each one of you will say mom did not teach me this. I did not know. There is nothing wrong with that because I too did not know. My hope and wish is that you will do good continually and come to truly love God the way I do, if not greater.

Always trust God and he will carry you through.

Always remember to have a relationship with God. Talk to him and be truthful to him. You can do this silently in your mind, through meditation or through silent prayer. By meditation I mean sitting down quietly somewhere and just talk to God quietly in your mind. Let your spirit connect with his.

Remember always no one, absolutely no one can tell you how to have a relationship with God. This is your relationship, your intimate moments with him.

Trust me many will tell you how, even say do things this way and that way but it is not your way it is their way so do not listen to them.

Another thing, under no circumstances must you turn from God.

What did I say?

Under no circumstances must you turn from God.

Do not infinitely do not let someone come to you with religion or tell you you have to be washed in blood in order to be saved. This is nastiness and the day you do God will turn from you because God does not deal in blood. A woman passed blood every 27-38. Yes thirty eight days but the 38 days comes later on in her life.

27-28 days is exact but there are times when it comes on the 38th day. I cannot explain this but know this to be true.

Trust God and be faithful and honest to God he will not let you down. So don't let anyone come and steer you wrong.

Don't worry I will know even when I am in my grave and trust me I will haunt any of you that turn from God and this I give you my word on.

Look around you and see the follies of this world, the hatred and killing. Why do you think it is there?

It is because our forefathers turned from God and today we are still doing it. Our forefathers did not listen, nor did we keep God's laws or commandments. Every time our ancestors did wrong and fall into the wrong hands they would cry to God. God would have mercy upon them and take them out of the situation, and as soon as God helped them, they spit in his face.

Much like some of the friends we help. As soon as you help them they turn against you. It's no different. It's like paying for a car and the person taking your money and you never get the car or the car is in such a bad shape it will cost you thousands of dollars to fix it.

Our forefathers were like this so eventually God said you know what I am tired of helping you out. None of you care about me, all you want to do is your own thing, follow after different gods, worship different gods and man, so do it. Let these Gods help you and do all that I do for you.

It is hurtful.

So I am telling you to think of God as well as his feelings because he does truly ove us all.

It is not fair for us to take him for granted.

It's not fair for him to do and we turn and spit in his face.

Today, we have no one to blame for our downfall. We have no one to blame for the condition of this world except for us, we ourselves.

Yes, God has sent help to get us back on track but all we have managed to do is to tell God we don't need his help because we can do things on our own.

So I am imploring all of you to walk in the good footsteps of God. Once you do this he will bless you as well as truly love you.

Also, know that when people see God blessing you they will try to hurt you because they will feel you are not worthy, they are more worthy than you. This is where jealousy steps in, jealousy on their part. I have taught all of you never to want what another man has nor go after what he has because none of you knows how he comes about it. ***Never ever be jealous of another man's possession but get your own.***

Be patient and wait on God to give you your good food.

My children know that man will promise you this and that but they will eventually fail you.

When you have children, dedicate those children unto the good service of God so

38

that they may cleave to Good and walk in his footsteps.

Know that there are physical and spiritual evil out there.

Spiritual evil is greater than physical evil because the spirit can go where the physical cannot go. The spirit has a lot of power. The power is so great at times that you will think you are going out of your mind; you will feel like you are going crazy and yes you will want to die. That is how great spiritual evil can be but call upon God and God alone. ***No one else but God.***

Know for a surety that no Man, no Pastor, no Spiritual healer, no one can help you but God. Meaning if God has not ordained that person he or she will never be able to help you.

Ask God to turn back the evil and release you from the dungeon that you are in and trust me within a day or two you will hear what God has done. ***This is why I tell you do not under any circumstance must you lift a finger or a hair to harm anyone.*** No matter what they do to you and your family trust God to work things out for you. ***This is what God wants and need. He needs you to trust him unconditionally. Love him unconditionally.***

My children put God at the head of your household as well as the head of your marriage and life.

Ask him to find the perfect mate for you.

Not just any mate but a truly loving and truly caring man or women.

A woman or man that is clean

A man or woman that do not follow the ways of the wicked

A man or woman that cleaves unto him - God

A man or woman that is there for you no matter what

A man or woman that will not lead you astray to follow unto false gods

A man or woman that will not lead you astray to worship idols

A man or woman that will not make you commit abominable acts of sin

A man or woman that will listen to God and take good council in his words

A man or woman that will truly love you for you and help you and God to raise

your children right according to God's true
love and laws

My children, when God has blessed you
with this person give him thanks and do
all in your power to represent God.

Cherish the gift that God has given you.

Do not abuse him or her

Let him or her know your goings and
comings

Take him or her with you at times

Take family vacations together

Have picnics together

Teach him or her all you know about God
and the respect of God so that when evil
people try to break you asunder they know
and cleave to God even more. Tell God
what that person is trying to do.

Never let evil people infiltrate your
peaceful household

If you know a person is evil as well as do
evil things do not walk in there way. Stay
clear of them

Remember when they see your
relationship going good and is blessed

from God know that they will try to split you up. They will bring dissension in your home.

Many will come in the name of God but trust no one but God. God will lead you and show you what he wants as well as need you to do.

Raise you children right

Scold them when they are wrong. Remember I made a lot of mistakes. Learn from them and do not do what I did.

Remember my good and the little that I do

Do goodness always

Do not put yourself in debt because of what your neighbor has

Do not let your wife or husband cause you to go into debt because of what your neighbor has.

Truly love what you have. If you have a car and it is running well, it gives no trouble keep it only when it starts to break down you invest in another one.

Never leave God for another god because the day you do you shall surely die. Eve left God and God told her she would die but she did not listen. Do not be like Eve listen to God.

Know that God does not kill if he did none of us on the face of this planet would be alive we would all be dead.

Never infinitely never ever let anyone tell you you have to die to get to God. Listen to me and hear me now my children never ever infinitely never ever let anyone tell you you have to die to get to God. This is an infinite lie. No one have to die to get to God because God is not dead he is alive. He is in everything. He in the air we breathe, the food we eat, the water we drink so do not be deceived by man or spirit. Teach your children this so that they know.

Never lie to your children

Never teach them to lie

Teach them to be honest at all times.

Teach them to be open with you at all times

Teach them about God

Teach them to always talk to God and make God their true friend in everything

Teach them to trust God and if they are
angry tell them to go to God with that
anger. They can be angry at God God will
not hold them sinful because they are
going to him with their problems.

Whatever they do not know tell them to
ask God and question him too. God does
not mind.

Teach your children to respect God at all
times.

Teach your grandchildren in the same
manner and commission your children to
teach their children in the like manner.

The reason why I say these things
especially leaving God is because of the
debt we are in.

Yes we are in debt. Thousands of years
ago someone told our ancestors to try
their gods, worship their idols because it
was easier. Their gods did not mind if they
fornicated, cheated, do all the things our
God told us not to do.

Our ancestors were told there gods was
better than our God and our ancestors
believed them. Man did they ever go astray
and today we are paying the penalty.

Instead of keeping the God they had, they
turned against him. Walked away from

peace, a peaceful way of life and it cost them dearly. It is still costing us.

Remember God is free; his love is good, blessings good; everything about God was good and is still good. We sold him. Gave him up and went for the other god. It was a costly price because today we still can't pay off our debt to these idols, and false god.

We go to this religion and that religion in hope of finding God. We listen to this Pastor and that Pastor and end up being confused, some of us go out of our minds; end up in the psychiatric ward. Some end up turning murders, vile human beings. Some of us turn prostitutes, rapist you name it we have become it.

See the thing is our ancestors never read the fine print, never asked any questions.

There eyes saw a bigger house, more land, saw a god that had no laws so why not jump in and they did.

Boy did they ever cry and we are still crying today. God told us we would die and we did die. Always remember the wages meaning the pay of sin is death.

You work and get your paycheque at the end of the week or two weeks depending how you work. Sin is the same way but your sins accumulate and turn into debt. Debt that we cannot repay because this is what we believe but this debt can be repaid. Meaning you can repay your debt and help others. It's not easy but over time you will comprehend. Meaning the good that you do repay your debt. Some sins cannot be repaid.

Listen and hear what I say. Some debts cannot be repaid no matter how much good you do. Let no one tell you God is merciful and he forgives all sin. Run dem and rebuke them in the name of God do you hear me.

Listen good GOD DOES NOT FORGIVE ALL SINS. Some sins that you commit you will never enter paradise you are just dead in the eyes of God. You are an abomination unto him. Yes worse than sin himself.

Know your sins and always admit when you are wrong like I've told you. No one can condemn you for admitting the truth not even God. This does not mean you will not be punished you will be punished because you know better. Accept the punishment. Serve it without complaint because you did do wrong. Once the sentence is over do not commit that sin again. Stay clear from it and stay clear from all sins. It is not easy but you know right from wrong so chose right at all times.

When you do wrong you are in debt in the physical and spiritual world and the thing that we do not realize and yes we have forgotten is that God does not put you in debt.

God does not put you in harms way

He is pure, kind and loving truly loving.

What our ancestors and us the people of today do not realize is that God never left us he is right here with us. He's the light, that beautiful feeling of love inside you when you find him. That feeling is so powerful at first that you feel as if you are going to explode. When you find God the evils of the world does not matter because you don't want to associate with those evil and wicked people. All you want to do is abide in God's arms and trust me it is safe, beautiful and secure.

This is why I say let no one make you turn from God. He is blessing you continue to cleave to him because once you get off track trust me the fall is great. It is hard to get back on board to God. Every manor of problems will hit you and hit you hard because he is gone. He will make you learn the hard way.

Your wife or husband will leave you

Bills will start to back up

Financial problems will hit you

Oh let's not mention the health problems that will face you

Everything will come upon you and trying to get back to him will be hard. It will be like climbing up a mountain. You know how tall and difficult a mountain is to climb. So if you are with God stay with him.

Also, never for one moment think that all will be well when you are dead. If you are against God in the living trust me you will be against him in death.

Remember a filthy person cannot under no circumstances enter into paradise. Let no man fool you and tell you about Jesus with the two thieves on the cross. You all know better. ***A FILTHY PERSON CANNOT AND WILL NEVER RESIDE PARADISE.***

You have to live a clean life.

You cannot say you love and hate your neighbor. It just does not work. You can hate the evil things he or she does but do not hate him. When he is ready to commit to God you will be surprised at how honest and blessed he or she will be.

Never try to change him or her. Talk only of the goodness of God.

Never use religion as your weapon because there is absolutely no religion in paradise. **_None_**. Only the love of God and babies, my children paradise is beautiful. It is splendid. A well kept garden that is beautiful to the eye does not do paradise justice. The light that is there is brighter than the suns rays. You can feel paradise within you because paradise is God and it is within you. It is in your genes.

My children I tell you all these things because I want and need you to know. I hope the explanation above did not confuse you but help you all.

Never live your life for greed. Hear me now and listen never live your life for greed because greed will kill you in the end. It is sinful.

Greed will cause you to go in debt

Greed will cause you to cheat

Greed will cause you to lie

Greed will cause you to kill

Greed will cause you to hate

Greed does cause jealousy because greed is one of the 24 evils – elders.

If your mate is greedy and follow after greed talk to them because greed will cause you to have nothing.

Always truly love what you do and be passionate about what you do.

My children you do not have to go to church to know God. If you are not comfortable with going to church do not go but praise, give thanks, sing to God, love him in the privacy of your own home because God did not give any church to man to worship him in.

The message I got on the school wall in my vision was 'FOR GOD SO LOVE US HE IS WORTHY TO BE PRAISED" and all this means is give him thanks. Think about him in the good and bad times. Be truly thankful for all that he has given unto you. Sometimes God is showing us things but because we lack proper communication the message is misguided so you have to know and learn what God is trying to tell you.

For example, you go to this store all the time and one day it is closed. Nothing is wrong with the store it's just closed. What

God is trying to tell you is that he does not want you to shop in that particular store. Find another store even if it is 50 miles away. Maybe the owner of the store is dirty, maybe they practice certain rights that is unlawful unto God. See God sees what we cannot see because he is way in the future. He's in a future time and this is his way of saying you are displeasing him meaning you are living a clean life and the owner of the store is unclean. When you shop in his store you are becoming unclean because he deals in unclean things. Always remember if a person is unclean nothing that he or she does can be clean. They have to clean themselves up.

So if you are unclean nothing that you do will be clean. It can only become clean unless you clean it up. It's much like going to the laundry. When your clothes is dirty do you not wash it? Well it's the same scenario.

Commit yourself to God in your home and let God baptize you and your children absolutely never ever let man baptize your child. This is a sin. Trust me infinitely it is a sin. People will say you have to be washed in water saved by the blood. God does not wash anyone in water. Never ever infinitely never ever forget this and I repeat God does not was anyone in water. Water is vital in the spiritual and physical world. When God is blessing you he showers you with water. He never washes you. Know this to be infinitely true water is what evil fears in the spiritual world. Evil cannot stand water know this and never forget it.

Hear me let God baptize you and your children because many that say they can baptize you, many that baptize have not a clean heart. Their hearts is as filthy more filthier than dung. When God baptize you you are well baptized. You are blessed.

This is why I tell you dedicate your children to God and all his goodness. Never say God I dedicate my child or children unto you. Say God I come before you with the gift of life you have given me – my child. God you have shown me the beauties of life as well as the beauties of you. In all I do I do it truthfully, honestly and it is with this truth and honest that I dedicate my child (name of child if you have one) unto your GOOD AND CLEAN service. God protect (name of child if you have one) and guide her/him in the right way. Teach them where I cannot teach them. Teach them truthfully and honestly of your honesty and truth. God never let them stray from you or follow in the pathway of evil. God every good work that needs to be done in your sight and in the sight of man let them do. Never let them do evil. I know they will make mistakes and I know mistakes are forgiven this is how they learn. I am trusting you to do all that is right and good by them and for them. Let them live a rewarding and prosperous life with you and wherever you reside. This I humbly and truly ask you as well as thank you (use your name).

My children the church is filled with many hypocrites, many that walk in the ways of evil.

Many of them do evil

Do not under no circumstances go in their way.

My children if you promise God you will not walk in the way of the wicked nor eat with them do not think that you will not be tested in the spirit and in the physical.

You will be tested both ways. Stand firm in the spiritual and physical. Live up to your word to God.

If you say God I will never go to church again do not go not even go in their parking lot because the parking lot belongs to the church and it is a part of the church. Trust me I learnt this and boy did I have it out with God. I could not concede with God but in the end I gritted me teeth and apologized to God. For those that will say this I say be careful because if you daughter or son say they want to be married in a church you cannot go because you gave your word to God and you have to live by it. Trust me God will not understand nor will he forgive you because you did give him your word. The reception you can go to, the park you can go to but you cannot go into the church or on its premises. If the reception is in the church all you cannot go. Remember funerals and weddings do not have to happen in a church.

Remember if your pastor or clergy is dirty meaning they are not clean your vows will not be clean so it is better you say them before God. Let the clergy person stand afar off and you say your vows to God and man meaning hold hands and say God I come before you in the sight of man and your angels and continue from there.

Temptation will come your way but resist

Always rebuke the enemy in the name of God. No other name but the name of God.

Call upon God and God only for rescue.

Ask him and only him to be your rock, your shield and protector.

No other God can protect you or shield you like God.

No other god can comfort you like God.

No other god can lift or will lift you to paradise like God.

God is the only one to call back the hands of the dead – the death angel

He's the only God that can and will commission the angels to heal you

The only God that can and will send his angels to comfort you, teach you

No other god or idol is as great as him.

They cannot do a thing. All they can do is put you in debt and cause you to go hungry and if you are not careful cause you to die.

Those other gods rob you of your birthright which is your soul

Look around you. How many families do each and every one of you know that has some problem or another. How many of them can't find money to buy food. Yes we've been broke but God always provide for us in some way. None of you can say mommy you are lying. We always had no matter how little it was we always had.

Forget about the broken furniture we always had a roof over our head and the rent was always paid no matter if I was a week or two late. We had it. Many can't say that.

No matter how little we had I was able to stretch fort my hand to family and friends back home.

All this was not my doing but God's doing.

He helped me to lend a helping hand and I am grateful for him. Grateful for what he did in my life and what he has shown me so take good council and listen to my words. The little my mother knew she taught me and I am teaching you. All four of you have taught me too. Good lessons and bad lessons.

Trust God to heal you and he will lead you to the right doctors. He will guide their hand in the operation room. He will take care of you. He will even send the right medicine to heal you. Send the right person to take care of you.

My children let no one tell you mommy or God don't love you. We both do. We both love all of you unconditionally.

My children cleave to your good mate.

Cleave to your good mate because God will never send you a bad mate.

Women and men will come and offer you everything. Better sex, better love, a better and bigger home, a truck load of happiness, they will say they are better looking, have a better shape, **_but run dem._**

Tell them to flee. Rebuke them in the name of God. All they give you is a bag of lies. They are like unto the false gods and idols of the days of old, the false gods and idols of today.

God have given you the jewels of paradise, the nectar of paradise why give that up for **_FOOLS GOLD._**

Do not go after them. When sex and love need a little spicing up in your life, spice it up with your wife or husband. Ask God to show you what you can do to spice it up and he will. You and your mate have a brain. Think of new ways to make love. **_Experiment with each other. Never ever go out of your marriage to seek pleasures because God does not like it. It is an abomination unto him._**

What did I say?

Never ever go out of your marriage to seek pleasures because God does not like it. It is an abomination unto him.

If you go outside your marriage to seek pleasure it is an abomination unto God.

These things my mother and grandmother did not teach me because they did not know.

I am just learning these things and I am teaching them to you.

Therefore not one of you can say well God mama never taught me because you have the book. All of you will have read this book at some point plus I have told you some of these things.

People will try to hurt you physically. Warn the person, tell them you are not going to beef with them or fight them.

Walk away and pray.

If they come to you with harm ask God to shield you and get the law involved. If you have to defend yourself defend yourself.

My children treat the family of your wife or husband with kindness

Never be miserly unto them. Do all that you can to help them but if they treat you poorly do not go in their way.

Treat your wife or husband with respect

Never feed him or her meats that are abominable unto God

Never give him or her vinegar to drink and say it is fine wine

Choose a name that represents God for your children

Never name them after false gods or false teachings. I did but I do not know. Remember my son you reminded me of respect and honor.

Remember heaven and hell is side by side but paradise reside within you

There are many laws that have been written but the greatest law of them all is true love – the true love of God.

Everything that God created was done out of truth – true love. He was passionate about his creation and the life he put upon this plain. He still is very passionate. He has so much love, care and mercy but it is man that has caused destruction to come upon us not God.

God does not kill man does. I know the bible says God told the people of old to kill. But the true God, the God of Love, My Darling and Love never ever killed anyone because he loves life and he is life. He loves to create and do things. **So let no** *book written and not written tell you that God kills because it is an infinite lie. I stand by my words, cling to God's words. Hear me because I cling to God's words not the words of men.*

Remember when God teaches you no man, woman or child can or will break you. They cannot fool you nor can they deceive you because you have been taught by God and God is the greatest teacher of all. Yes I've told him he's a lousy teacher but he knows why and he is correcting himself in my words.

Also remember KNOWLEDGE IS A GIFT FROM GOD. USE IT WISELY.

NEVER USE THE KNOWLEDGE THAT GOD HAS GIVEN YOU TO LIE, CHEAT AND DECEIVE.

USE THE KNOWLEDGE OF GOD TO DO GOOD ALL THE TIME.

HELP OTHERS HONESTLY WITH IT.

The reason why I tell you this is because I have seen first hand how man can use knowledge to deceive and get what they want.

Yes it sickened me and all I could say to that person was "thank you, you taught me a valuable lesson." He asked why but I didn't tell him of the lies he told all I said again was "just thank you."

See when God wants you to learn certain things he will make you learn it. You might go away on vacation and see certain things or just be in your workplace and he shows you certain things. He is showing you how not to act at times, how to act, how not to judge. *All that he needs you to learn he will show you. Teach you and all of you make sure you teach your children and bring them up in the ways of God and not the ways of man.*

My children know that for all that I did not teach you or show you God will teach and show you. He will take care of you, protect you.

My children always do the goodness that God tells you to do.

Never go after false gods, idols, friends or walk in the way of the wicked and don't think for one moment that you won't have family members that are not wicked. Some are wicked too and walk in the way of the wicked, but do not worry God will show you the right one.

Remember, always his angels are there to guide you and if you feel something is wrong then something is wrong.

If you are sitting down and you feel a tug on your shirt or skirt and you look around and no one is there. <u>Get up do not sit in that seat.</u> God is telling you to move something is going to happen.

Listen to me and move I didn't and ended up getting vomit on me.

If you are doing something wrong trust me God will tell you so stop doing it and repent. I am speaking from experience. I was doing something wrong and the voice said to me "what you are doing is wrong." I did not listen and plugged along. For two nights the angels of God came to me and trust me I was not happy but I conceded because they were there to warn me.

Trust me you don't want the angels of God hurting you. Not pretty so take heed.

The angels are real. God don't send them for nothing. He sends them for a cause and they cannot and will never tell God no. So listen to my good council.

If you find my words wrong GO TO GOD AND NOT MAN. I REPEAT GO TO GOD AND NOT MAN. I DON'T CARE IF YOU SAY GOD MY MOM HAS GONE CRAZY BUT WHAT SHE SAID IS IT TRUE. GOD WILL ANSWER YOU JUST GIVE HIM TIME.

Remember, the physical, our time is different from spiritual time.

The spiritual world is further ahead of us.

Physical time have to catch up to it that is why at times we do not get answers to what we ask right away.

Sometimes we say God is slow but he is sure.

God is not slow he is right on time.

Our time or earthly time is slow, lagging behind.

So remember spiritual time and physical time are not the same. They were once the same do not get me wrong but because of our actions the two have separated we have lost that connection. It's not to say we can't get it back we can and the way to do this is to be totally honest and clean with God. Don't lie to him. LOVE him TRUTHFULLY.

When you do trust me even the shoes you buy, the underwear you wear you will want him to choose and buy for you.

Everything becomes different, and can become perfect. Like I said you will see the happening in the world and just want to stay in your little corner with God. You don't make it concern you. He shields you from the wickedness that is out there. He shields you from the stress because you no longer worry about the pleasures of the world you are becoming in tune with him.

It's not to say you don't pay your bills. Pay them because you have to maintain your family and credit. I don't know how to explain it properly. It's like you just want to be surrounded by your wife and kids.

You want to do things with them only.

Your family is your friends and God is at the forefront.

You will even want to go out on dates with God, take a vacation with him and he will because he will be right there with you.

You may not be able to see him but you can feel him. How, you may feel a cool breeze tingle you and bring a smile to your face. Well that's God.

You may get a smile from a perfect stranger, that's his way of saying I am with you.

He will guide your plane and put it down safely. (This he will show you plainly).

When it comes to God you will feel as if you are in a different world and nothing matters but him. Your life is going great, you are communicating with him, talking to him and he is listening.

On the days when you want to have a date with him do it. Get a bowl of fruits and cuddle up in your bed and watch your favorite movie with him.

Trust me you will end up eating all the fruits and when you realize it you will say God I ate all the fruits and laugh saying you were greedy.

Don't believe me try it and know.

In all you do give God all the respect.

Do not treat him like he's not there because he is there with you.

Do not alienate him out of your life because he does not alienate you.

He is kind and merciful and if he wasn't trust me he would have withdrawn the sun a long time ago. You all know we cannot live without the sun we would die without it. Our bodies need heat. Plants need heat. We all need God and God is the sun as well.

Learn your lessons well my children and remember:

LOVE GOD TRUTHFULLY

BE TOTALLY HONEST WITH HIM

CLEAVE TO HIM

BE LIKE STATIC CLING TO HIM

WHEN PEOPLE TRY TO THROW YOU OFF HOLD ON TO HIM

NEVER EVER LET GOD GO BECAUSE IF YOU DO YOU WILL BE DOOMED

DESTRUCTION WILL BE UPON YOU AND TRUST ME IT WILL BE LIKE CRYING TIME ALL OVER AGAIN. YOU WILL CRY AND IT WILL BE HARD TO GET HIM BACK. IT WILL BE LIKE LOSING A LOVED ONE. THE PAIN AND SORROW IS GREAT.

IN ALL YOU DO

DO IT OUT OF TRUE LOVE - TRUTH

DO IT OUT OF THE TRUE LOVE OF GOD

Never ever infinitely never ever marry a man or woman for their money this is a sin and your love is not true. This is hate

Whatever you do do not disrespect God.

Live by Psalms 1 when it said blessed is the man that walketh not in the council of the ungodly. Do not walk in the council of the ungodly. They are wicked and evil and they will cause you to turn from God. Read Proverbs by Solomon and hear what he said because he too turned from God and committed abominable acts in the sight of God. God loved him truly loved him but because of lust, greed he strayed and lost his soul to other women that practiced idolism as well as worshipped idols.

Do not buy any goods from the ungodly

Do not eat in their homes, schools, restaurants. Any place where the ungodly convene do not go there or eat there. They are evil. Do not go against God. Listen to God because God too will protect you so that you do not eat from them or go into their place to buy their goods.

Do not go in the lands of the ungodly. God never sent any of his messengers into the lands of the ungodly. Some may say Egypt was ungodly but no Egypt was never ungodly meaning good and evil was separated but evil got in the back door. The devil's clan had to conquer Egypt because the books of life was housed there. Meaning the Ying and Yang was housed in Egypt and that was why Moses went into Egypt. He had to take life out of Egypt and free God's people from slavery because the devil's clan did enslave God's people. The polluted the land so God had to take life out lest we all died. Meaning you nor I would be here today. Evil did get hold of some of the books but the important one they did not get because evil cannot open that book nor look upon it. That book belongs to God and no man can open it because it is sealed by God. Yes this is the book that Revelations talked about.

With God's book no one can use it for evil. The books that were in Egypt were important because evil used them to do evil. They used them for enchanting – witchcraft. Voodoo, Obeah. The bible that we read, this book that man say is divinely inspired is used for evil and used in evil so therefore it cannot be of God nor is it divinely inspired.

Remember God do tell us whom to marry and who to lay with so never ever absolutely never ever infinitely never ever marry a babylonian or take them into your land not because of race but because of the lies they have told on God.

They caused Eve to lose her soul. This man told Eve she would not die and she did die. Basically he called God a liar and she believed him and trust me it cost her her life. The lie is so great that man every race on the face of this planet have bought into this lie and is now living by this lie.

Trust no Babylonian nor go in the way of any Babylonian because they are cunning and deceitful. They know they have no part and parcel in God's kingdom so do not go amongst them. Honor and respect God because good and evil were separated in the beginning.

Good and evil must separate in the end.

Listen to me and hear me keenly do not marry any Babylonian. It has nothing to do with race but it has everything to do with their vile and sinful ways. THE GREAT LIE THEY TOLD ON GOD. Trust none of them

They hate God with a passion and this is why they are doing all in their power to make you defile God. They use race as their bargaining chip and this is why every race under the face of the run including our own hate black people. Nothing good comes from them. They will use your own people to deceive and kill you and they are doing it. Try you best not to befriend them nor live amongst them.

Infinitely remember this God judges no one nor is God racist. God sees what you cannot see. He knows what you don't know. Yes we could get mad at God for creating evil but it was never so. Everything was created good but the origins of man changed over time. Life before man walked the earth was perfect and good. There was no strife nor were these beings fleshy. They were pure energy meaning they were spiritual beings and void of flesh and this is why the human eye and the spiritual eye cannot see them.

Always remember the devil's seed know the more man sin and bask in sin the further away God gets.

They know just how clean God is. God cannot come in nor can he reside in a dirty home or planet so the more we kill and sin the more God stays away and the more humanity and the universe die. Meaning all life whether air, trees, birds, water dies. Everything becomes polluted.

Trust me their words are sweeter than fine wine but the heart is deadlier than a black widow spider.

They are that cunning and deceitful.

Do not fight them because they are the masters of war and strife. No one can win the devil in his domain always remember this. I repeat no one can win the devil in his domain this is why I tell you do not fight them. Do not allow evil in your domain. The day you let evil in is the day you have lost control because evil will and does dominate and they will kill you if they cannot get their way. Trust me they will use their people as human shields to get their own way so stay away from them.

Do not put yourself in debt for them meaning do not fight your battles for them. If they enlist you for help charge them for your services and never ever let them hold you or your country accountable for deaths incurred in their land. Be clear with your contract with them because this contract is binding and let that country that enlist your help pay for the deaths you incur meaning that country must take care of that soldier's family for life yes this includes medical expenses and schooling for that soldier's children. Any needs that child or family need it must be met by that country and vise versa. If you enlist the help of other nations and death is incurred then you to are responsible for that soldier's family you and or your country must maintain upkeep of that soldier's family for life. This is the law and no man can break God's law. God did not tell any man to kill or go to war against his or her neighbor evil is the one to do say so meaning tell lies on God for you to believe. Do not worry yourself about evil because his pay is death and evil must and will die for the wrongs he and his people have committed.

Protect your borders at all cost do you hear me and never forget if you do not allow evil in your land they cannot come in. Evil use immigration to get in and once they are in they wreak upon your land. They drain it and leave your people destitute and land destitute. They enslave and enact their laws and say it is of God. God does not enslave know this. Evil enslaves not God and no evil has a right to come in and enslave your people or take your land. Have strict immigration polices within your land meaning do not take the food out of the mouth of your people and give it unto others. This is a sin. Think of the people of your homeland and always do good unto them. If you are the overseer for your people make sure they have good food to eat at all times and make sure they have shelter meaning a good roof over their heads because they are depending on you for many things and their good and safe well being is one of them.

It's not to say God does not protect his people. God does protect his people. If you are living by God and doing all the good that God tells you to do evil cannot harm you. They cannot conquer your land. God will shield you. The only way evil can conquer you is if you let them in. Evil is like a vampire. Think of evil in this sense the sense of a vampire. A vampire cannot come into your home unless he or she is invited. Once they are invited in what do they do? They take your life and this is what evil does. It takes your life by sucking the life out of you. So know evil and stay away from evil.

Do not hate them because the Babylonians are not one specific race of people anymore and this is because of sin and the terrible acts of sin that we commit. We married sin and do all that is sinful and this is what Eve and the people of the garden did. They married sin. Those that refused were enslaved and killed. Now you will find the Babylonians have mixed with every race on the face of the planet. This was their way of getting into God's kingdom so because of this they can get in by truth and honesty only. Even though they have intermarried with the different races they cannot get in just like that they too have to live a clean and honest life.

They have to break away from sin and prove to God they are worthy.

Know that it was because of what they did they don't have any part and parcel in God's kingdom but this is the choice they made with their lies and deceit. This goes for anyone that knowingly commits sin and partakes in sin.

Because we married sin sin has become a part of our genes – our genetic makeup. I did not know this until recently so hear me now and ask God to take the sinful gene (s) from your genetic makeup. Ask him for forgiveness and plead with him because you did not know. Plead with him to take the sinful gene (s) from your children and grandchildren. Tell him to take it permanently in a good way from any genetic off springs that may come from your bloodline. If God refuse this your plea then yes you can hold God guilty of sin.

Know that the only three race that I saw on God's mountain were Chinese and Blacks on the first level

The second level Whites resided there and it was not many whites, I only saw one male and he looked sickly. I did not see the inside of his abode so I do not know how many more they were.

The third level or top level I saw only Blacks. The only races that I did not see were the Indians and Spanish or Japanese. I am not spreading hate but this is how I saw it in my vision and this is how I am relaying it to you. It's not to say Indians cannot get to God's abode. They can but they have to be clean and honest. Also remember and infinitely never forget this. Good people in the spiritual realm meaning good people that reside in God's abode is represented by black people. Never forget this.

White people that are good you are black in God's abode

Black people and it does not matter if you are mixed as long as you are good you are black in God's abode

Chinese if you are good you are black in God's abode

For better clarity refer to the Ying and the Yang. One is white and the other is black.

The white represent spiritual death. Meaning anyone that is evil they die as a white person clothed in full white in the spiritual realm. Know that this is for those that have totally given themselves over to evil. Anyone that is good becomes black in the spiritual realm – they go on to God's abode. Do not be confused by this because if you have loved one that has passed away you will see them in their original form meaning if they were white you will still see them as white if they visit you and vise versa.

For some races they use the Blue and the White Nile or Blue and White.

Blue is a very powerful colour in the spiritual realm. Evil in the spiritual realm is represented by Blue and good is represented in the spiritual world as White but that is only in colour not in skin. The correct infinite correct analogy is the Ying and the Yang. This is the infinite truth so let no one tell you otherwise.

Know this also. Those that are clothed in blue are also teachers. They teach you about sin. They are very powerful so know them and do not be deceived by them.

Anyone that hates black people and white people hate themselves because this is how the universe and man was made up. We were all made from the Ying and the Yang. Good and Evil. Each one of us is capable of good and evil – both.

Never marry love marry true love – truth because the truth cannot lie but love lies all the time.

I can say a Babylonian will never see God's abode but I would be lying because God does not exclude anyone from his abode. Yes the Babylonians are evil and vile and it is because of their vile and dirty ways they are locked out but the now generation can change this but they have to be truthful honest and true to God. They must live clean and abandon all forms of evil and wickedness.

Remember God knows the heart of the wicked but the heart of the good and pure he infinitely loves and adore

Always remember the sins you do define who you are and this goes for the good that you do as well. Meaning your goodness define who you are as well

We all say God judges including me but I have learnt that God does not judge. He cannot judge you based on the good or the bad that you do because sin is automatic death there are no ands ifs or buts about it.

Good is life eternal

Like I have said there are sins that are forgiven and there are sins that are not forgiven no matter the good that you do.

Know that we all have a birth certificate and a death certificate and this depends on you. Yes some do not have a death certificate only a birth certificate but like I said this all depend on the person and the life they live on earth.

If you live a nasty and vile life on earth you cannot live a good and clean life in the afterlife.

Always remember the life you live on earth determines where you go in the spiritual or afterlife.

Always remember no man can go into hell on his or her own. If a man or woman tell you they have been to hell question them? If they said God brought me there or an angel brought him or her there know that that person is a damned liar.

A child of God cannot go to hell just like that without being changed. They have to change. Meaning God's angels change them and shield them from the wickedness of hell. This I know to be infinitely true.

If a man or woman say no man has seen God refer them to Job, Eve, Moses

If they say Moses saw a burning bush as the bible say tell them I say they are a damned liar because God does not use fire nor is there fire where God resides.

And yes the bible is inaccurate infinitely inaccurate

And no hell hath no fire either and yes the bible is infinitely incorrect

The fire in hell meaning the containment unit that will house Satan and his people is like unto atomic fire. Meaning the hue is a pinkish purplish hue. It is not fire fire as man would have you believe.

Therefore know that the hue of spiritual fire is pinkish purplish. Let no man tell you otherwise. This is how God showed it to me and this is how I am telling you and will show you if you ask.

Do not eat the meat of swine and say it is good meat it is unclean and an abomination unto God.

Know infinitely know the food of choice in the spiritual realm for both good and evil is chicken and yes this is why evil use the blood of chicken to invoke the dead. Chicken is predominantly used by evil. It is their sacrifice unto the dead. It's death's pay or payment. In time hopefully you will comprehend this.

It is not all meat is good to eat. But never eat the meat of a swine – pork it is unlawful unto God. Yes an abomination.

Not all fish is good to eat so know the fish that is lawful unto you. My choice of fish is Red Snapper this my body can tolerate all others my body cannot. So know which fish is right for you. The fish I eat may not be right for you. Some people's body can tolerate King Fish, Mackerel, Salmon, this is lawful for them but not lawful for me because of my body and what it is telling me. Sometimes you have to listen to your body because the food that is right for me may not be right for you. I eat salt fish – cod fish for those who know it as cod fish but it's not all cod fish that taste the same. Some people's body can tolerate salt fish and some people's body cannot. Yes this is branding and where the fish is from. Stay away from Eels they are unlawful do not eat them or let anyone prepare them for you. Remember the meat of swine never ever infinitely never ever eat it and never forget to read the label because some food contain pork. Yes my pet peeve with grocery stores is that they mix the too. Meaning put meats that are unlawful beside meats that are lawful. Whenever possible shop for meats in stores that do not sell pork but that's impossible because all stores sell pork.

A lot of people eat pork this is lawful for them but it is not lawful for you so do not eat it. Stay away from it. God does not allow this for his people so infinitely stay away from this meat. The meat of a swine or pigs is used in the highest form of evil. It is that disgusting. Know that when God is showing you something bad is going to happen to you the fat of pork is used meaning pork fat.

God will also show you pigs in the person's yard with Aloes. The aloes are tall giants and the back yard is dirty with some of the aloes it could be one of the aloe sliced down the middle meaning you can see the belly of the aloe. This means stay away from this person and their family because they say they are good meaning they are healers but in actuality they are demons. They work iniquity – they are not clean.

Aloe and pineapple in clear river water is good know this but planted and around pigs this is true evil – filth.

Infinitely stay away from the carcass or meat of unclean animals this is infinitely unlawful unto God.

Also remember not all fruits are good to eat. Try to eat fruits with seeds at all times.

Stay away from engrafted fruits if you can meaning manmade fruits. Organic food and fruits is the way to go because God gave humanity – human and beast – animals organic food to cat. God never gave humanity chemically induced food to eat. Everything God gave to us is good not bad.

Keep your body and home clean at all times

Do not practice your children to go from home to home meaning do not practice them to go to friends homes all the time because you do not know the hearts of people and what they might do. Meaning not all parents are parents some dabble in unlawful things

Yes we all need friends but make God your true friend. God is my true friend so are all of you. You were and still are my friend. Yes I drove you all crazy and drove God crazy too but this is the way I want and need it to be.

Cherish the home that God has given you because it is well given.

Know that living right is not easy but take it one day at a time and always know that tomorrow comes for everyone

If you cut one tree down replant two (2) or three (3) in its steed because you never know which one will grow.

Never forget that evil hates God with a passion and will do anything in its power to kill life – good.

Evil destroys everything in its path this is because evil hath no part and parcel like I've said with God so it will destroy everything including you.

Evil does cause humanity to sin so do your best to suppress sin by thinking of God and his goodness at all times.

Evil must die he knows this and because he knows this and this is why evil is so revengeful. He will cause all of humanity to go down with him. Everything that hath life he will destroy and he is doing it today. Humanity is destroying all including self and no one wants to change or see this.

We destroy the air we breathe by polluting it with harmful chemicals and carbons without thinking that we need air to sustain and maintain life

We pollute and destroy the water without thinking that we need it to maintain and sustain life

We destroy the trees – forests without thinking that the trees clean the air we breathe. We refuse to admit that trees maintain and sustain life

We destroy the earth by shedding blood and polluting the ground with harmful chemicals. Chemicals that get into the food we eat. Chemicals that are slowing kill us by giving us cancer and other forms of disease and ailments.

We destroy and kill each other therefore shutting our soul/spirit out of God's kingdom – abode.

We alter self due to vanity and none know that when we alter self there is no forgiveness for this.

Know that when a man or woman change their sex to become another God never forgives them. There is no forgiveness for this abominable sin.

Keep your birth certificate in tact because this is your life lesson meaning your life.

Your birth certificate is vital in life. Yes vital in both worlds meaning the spiritual and physical world.

Never change your sex like the heathens do because they are loathsome in the sight of God and man.

If your child is born a male indicate it on his birth certificate

If your child is born a female indicate it on her birth certificate

If your child is born an imorphadite indicate it and chose the correct gender for him or her. If he has more of a male genitalia make him male. If his genitalia is more of a female make her female. This will be hard to do so seek God's help and he will help you.

Never change your birth certificate. Your gender is your gender and it is unlawful to change it. There is no forgiveness of sin for this no matter the goodness that you do.

If your child is born a male and at a certain point in their life they change to female due to genetics meaning they did not get surgery keep the original birth certificate male because he was born a male. This must be a natural occurrence and void of any interference from man and spirit including nature.

Do not change your laws to accommodate sin because God cannot change his laws to accommodate or suit you.

Know that it is unlawful for a man or woman to change his sex in the eyes of God. It is also unlawful in the eyes of man – humanity.

Know the truth of Sodom and Gomorrah.

Know that these people are the true Sodomites.

Do not let God loathe and despise you because of them because they have no rights in the sight of God and man.

They willingly and knowingly cause you to commit anus crimes of sin against God. They claim that they are males and females when they know that they are not. Some were born as a male and some were born as a female. They cannot change their birth certificate to say otherwise this is unlawful and sinful unto God. This is infinite disrespect on their part and for this there is no forgiveness of sin because they went against God and the laws of God.

They are liars and an abomination of sin. They are worst than Satan and to man Satan is the lowest of them all.

They are things and unlawful in the sight of God.

Any man or woman that lay with them is also guilty of sin because they know that they did wrong.

Even if you do not know these things meaning you engage in a relationship with them against your knowledge you are guilty of sin because they caused you to lay with them and for this there is no forgiveness or remission of sin.

There is absolutely nothing that you can do to correct this – infinitely nothing so know who you lay with and pick up. Your soul is at stake do not lose it for unlawful and abominable sin.

Anyone that knowingly commit this act of sin meaning lure you in their unlawful ways death is their reward. They must be put to death in God's court meaning the death that is outlined for evil will not be the death that these people face it will be far worse.

Satan has done a lot of wrongs yes but this sin is beneath Satan because not even him is this grand and bold to disrespect God and his laws in this way. This is why I have said there are greater sins meaning a greater evil than Satan and what you know of the days of old.

No the containment unit that will house Satan will not house them because they truly and knowingly defileth God.

None of them like I've said have no right to God so they do not have any rights before man.

Know that spiritual death is harsher than physical death meaning the death of skin which is the flesh.

Know that the spirit is what keeps the skin or flesh alive because the skin is the conductor or house for the spirit – soul.

Stay out the lands of Sodom and Gomorrah because they partake in the lies and deceit of sin and they infinitely disrespect and dishonor God.

Vacation not in their lands nor eat their food.

Do not take none of their women or men to marry because when you do this you are disrespecting God because these people have none for God.

Do not uphold and partake in their slackness and nastiness. God gave you all that is good he never gave us anything that was unlawful or disrespectful.

Even if the people of this land cry until blood comes out do not disrespect God and have anything to do with them. If you do you are condoning sin and this in itself is unlawful and death in God's eyes. You will trust me infinitely on this you will be contained in the same containment unit as them – you will die harsher than death and let no one tell you that this is not so because it is so.

Man loveth all that is sinful and hateth all that is good – God.

You now know the vile acts of sin that these things commit do not befriend them nor partake of anything with them.

As for transvestites meaning men that dress in drag God does not hate you for this because you are performing an act and as women we do dress as men for example the pants. What is unlawful and abominable unto God is going against the laws of God by getting operations – changing your sex to become male or female and saying you are a male or female when you know that you were not born this way.

No one can change their birth or death certificate it is unlawful and wrong.

Any parent that condone this is wrong. Yes you can argue that it is your body and you have a right to do whatever you want to with it. Then tell God. Go to God and tell him this then exit off this planet. Create one that is suitable for you because not of you have no right on this planet because none of you created it. This is God's planet and sin have no right on it. You want an abode for yourself create one and get the f off earth. Plain and straight you cannot do wrong and expect to get right. You cannot disrespect God and live in his abode. No if you hate yourself and God so much let evil true evil – SHE – create a planet for you and go there and live.

Why should you disrespect God like this and please do not tell me about you felt as if you were born in the same body. Bullshit. Not even Satan has tried that shit.

You all have a land now that has given you all the rights to practice as things go there. Live there or like I said get the F off the planet earth because you are polluting the planet in a devastating and evil way.

Go back to Sodom because all of you are vile and disgusting.

My children hate no one and yes above sound hateful but my spirit gets upset when it comes to certain things and God. I cannot explain the reason as to why my spirit gets cross and upset. Sometimes I say I am feeling what God feels when I am writing. When you truly come to love God – truly love God you will comprehend this. I do not hate these people and I do leave them to God and time but do not follow them or be in their company. Always remember God is both male and female meaning in the physical God is female but Male in the spiritual and he does interchange but this he God himself will show you and teach you. If you are at a loss look at the male gene XY meaning x represent female and Y represent male.

Never hate anyone based on sexual orientation meaning do not follow the heathens and say God hates Homosexual because there are homosexuals in paradise.

God cannot hate you based on truth but he can hate you based on lies.

Remember never go outside of your relationship for pleasure. This is sinful and an abomination unto God.

Teach your children to be clean at all times. Remember my struggles with cleanliness when it came to all of you.

Keep your body clean at all times and yourself clean at all times. Teach your children this as well

Keep away from loud men and women they are sorrowful to the soul

Cherish the quiet because it is only when you are quiet can you hear what God is saying to you

Never ever infinitely never ever let anyone tell you you have to die in order to find God. God is the true love within you that beautiful feeling inside of you. When you feel it you will comprehend what I am saying and telling you.

Always listen to soothing and good music because it is pleasant to the soul. It calms your raging spirit.

Always enjoy life and take time out for you. Teach your children this as well.

Let no one give you blood to drink whether physical or spiritual. This is an abomination unto God. It is sinful and it is automatic death.

Always remember God is life and no one has to die to acquire life because we all have it. It is life that maintains and sustains good and evil

Know and infinitely know that God never used anyone as a sacrificial lamb to save humanity. No one can die to save you nor did God commission anyone to die for you or anyone. If God commissioned this he would be going against his own law. He would be sinful and yes he would be a liar and a deceiver – no better than skin and sins sinful and deceitful people.

Infinitely know that the good that you do on earth is what saves you in the afterlife – death.

Infinitely know that God does not deal in animal or human sacrifices. These things are of the devil. It is sinful and an abomination unto God. Animal and human sacrifices are the pagan and Babylonian way. Do not practice it nor follow them because they hate you and hate God even more. They will do all to destroy life and this is what they are doing so always be mindful of them.

Do not hate them because God did not keep them out of his abode because of their skin tone it was because they were wicked and deceitful. They were liars and they are still liars.

Like I've said everyone can reach God's abode but we have to be clean, truthful and honest to God.

Do not I repeat do not commission the moon nor seek help from the moon in anything because the moon is a reflection of war and death. Do you hear me? Do not commission the moon nor seek help from the moon because it is a reflection of death. Meaning the moon is spiritual death. War and strife begin on the moon and this is why man seek to get there. It is a place of war. It is void of life meaning good life. It is filled with death meaning war starts on the moon before it comes to earth. See it and know it because there is no peace on the moon. Yes the moon represents many things but the one thing that man do not know and that is the true nature of the moon. The war and strife within and yes the technology not yet known to man.

Know that in the beginning man could not die it was when we allowed sin into our lives we begin to die.

Know that death must die but life can never die and this is why I say live for life and never live for death.

Always infinitely always stay on the pathway of God because God is the truth and he is life everlasting. He is also that beautiful mountain that man keep running from. Never run from the mountain because the mountain is significant. Know that the mountain is God so never let go of the mountain – never let go of God.

Remember evil must kill to maintain and sustain his life. He must make you sin and do all that is sinful to keep him going. If everyone was to live truthfully and honestly sin would cease to exist all together.

Never seek what sinful and wicked people have. Remember never fight anyone but leave them to God and time. Infinitely remember time is the key to life and death. It is the key to everything including evil. Never forget evil only lives for a time but good is life eternal so live for life.

Remember it is the flesh that dies in the physical but the spirit lives on. Man do not know about life after death because man cannot see beyond death.

Do not let anyone tell you that life is recycled in the spiritual. Life is not recycled. Good moves on to better and greater life but evil dies. It must die it cannot continue on.

Remember evil will forever terrorize the earth because humanity made it so. As long as we are living in sin on earth evil spirits will remain.

These spirits are the ones to cause havoc on humanity.

Let no one tell you this is not so and that this is a lie. It is so. God cannot lie nor will he lie to any of you.

Always seek God in truth and he will show you all in truth. Let no man tell you to do otherwise.

Do you hear me? Seek God in truth and he will show you all in truth. Meaning God will show you the truth.

Do not be like the heathen and say it is not so. Infinitely remember and know that God does not lie and he will never lie to anyone and he will never lie to you. The heathens will tell you that you have to die but hear me and listen to me you do not have to die. If humanity had to die all God would have to do is take away the air, food and water. That's all God would have to do but he does not he keeps it all for us to see his goodness and mercy. Like I said God is life and he cannot kill if he did he would be a liar and deceiver. He would be sinful so do not listen to the heathens with their lies because they are the same one that said God had as son that died for us. This is a lie. I told you God will never send anyone to sacrifice their lives for sinful and wicked people nor would he send anyone to sacrifice their lives for good people. Good people do not have to worry about their souls only wicked and evil people does because they have no part and parcel within God's kingdom. They know that which is right but they continuously do evil – wrong.

Infinitely remember and never forget this and teach this to your children. If you have dedicated a place of worship to God make sure you take off your shoes before you enter the sanctuary. Do not be like the heathens that trample down God and say they are worshipping and praising him. Trust me infinitely they are hated by God. And I use hate for lack of a better word.

If God is holding your hand never let go of his hand. Do you hear me? If God is holding your hand never let go of his hand because the day you do you will regret it.

If your neighbor have a huge house do not be jealous of him nor want to be like him. Never be red eye for another man's property or anything of his for that matter.

Be satisfied with what you have because humanity live for greed. They are the ones to bankrupt their country then turn around and curse their heads of state. Never be like them because they are the heathens of society. They want it all and when they get it all they turn against you when the economy is bad. No one sees their greedy and glutinous because they want everything today and forget about tomorrow. They have not hearts they would rather bankrupt you and the country instead of securing their future and saving some for tomorrow. They would rather leave the future high and dry because they have no thought for future generations, their children and grand children.

They are the ones that have but say they have not. They need more so they put pressure on everyone and anyone.

If you have a company or if you are elected leader of a country never run it based on greed and never cheat Caesar out of his dues. The day you do you will regret it. Everyone wants to cheat Caesar and many do so do not be like the many. Pay your dues to Caesar because as bad as it may seem some of the money Caesar collect go into running the country. The one thing you must hold firm to is your Pension. Never let Caesar cheat you of this nor let Caesar give some of your portion to other people. If you are elected leader of any country secure the peoples pension because they are entrusting their future to you. Meaning they are trusting you to have their backs when they grow old and cannot work. Your pension is your right. Their pension is their right. This is your entitlement a part of your birthright and Caesar has no right to rob you or them of this. Caesar told you he wants this much each pay to help him run the country and you willingly give this to him. He cannot rob you of your pension you worked hard for this and he cannot rob you of that. This is wrong on Caesar's part because you are not robbing him.

When it comes to the sick and elderly ensure they have proper health care meaning if they require medicines do not say they are not entitled to it. As a leader ensure that pharmaceutical companies invest in the health care of the elderly. It can be by donating free drugs to help them because they did buy your pills. Pills that were to help them but caused other health defects. No the pharmaceutical companies are not to blamed for all health ailments because sin and evil impacts us all in a negative way meaning we do things to impact ourselves negatively. Everything that we do meaning to signal out one member of the industry would be wrong and sinful because some food we eat have negative health impact, the gasoline that we put in our cars affect us and the environment, the electricity we use impact our waterways and environment, the sewer system that we use impact the food we eat, our drinking water and the environment, the chemicals that we use on our food impact our body and the environment and all in a negative way so to single out one particular company would be wrong and unlawful – sinful. We can make better choices and some of those choices are:

Organic food
Bio diesel
Plant Corn and Sugar grade Oil
Organic clothing instead of synthetic
Recycled paper
Recycled cars

Recycled houses
Recycled wood and wood shavings

We can do more to improve and secure our future but it takes every nation on a global scale.

Right now earth need to replenish its resources but man have yet to see this but you know it so do your part to help the environment and trust me the earth and God will bless you.

Caesar cannot say well X amount of people needed the pension. Caesar cannot say that because you gave him taxes to accommodate for those people. Your pension is your pension. If person x came into the country and he has not contributed to the government pension or any pension then he or she is not entitled to any of yours. This is yours. He is entitled to pension from his country of origin meaning if he lived in Germany for 55 years and he worked their he is not entitled to your pension he is entitled to the pension from his country of origin and he must collect pension from his country of origin. If he or she did not work then his family that sponsored him or her they are responsible for that person. Your pension is yours and no one else's and no one can protest this because right is right and wrong is wrong. You cannot be wrong and get right this is not fair. If a person is disabled and cannot work then Caesar cannot deny them pension because you gave Caesar money to help and this is called Federal Tax. And no you cannot be disabled in your country of origin and expect to get disability in my country. Your country of origin is responsible for you. Right is right and fair is fair. They cannot take from a system that they have not contributed to come on now.

Never be like the heathens and overly produce then watch the balance go bad. Never overly produce if you can help it. Produce what the market demands and need nothing else. Always remember tomorrow and secure your company's or country's future.

If you are entrusted with leadership for your country never treat a thief differently from a murderer. Do you hear me never treat a thief any different from a murderer both acts are equally sinful and unlawful.

Never cater to the hardened criminal but let them do hard labour to earn their keep.

If the jail grounds have enough land fence it around and let them plant provisions. They can sell these provisions for money but they have to pay rent for the upkeep of the jail or prison. All that they need they must buy and cannot credit. If they take a life they are indebted to the family of that slain victim they must pay restitution for life because they did take a life. If the family does not require restitution then they cannot pay for restitution because none is required of them. A portion of the money they earn must go towards their family also so if the pay of each inmate is $20.00 per day than them money is shared equally for rent, the prisoner, his family and the family he or she owes restitution to. If he makes $100.00 per week nothing changes equal share for all all around.

Be mindful of the children if a family cannot handle their child and gives that child to the state then the state is responsible for that child until he or she comes of age to be on their own.

If am a man seduces a young child he or she must face the consequences of 100 lashes and jail time. Plus incur all medical bills and he or she is indebted to that child for life because he did do wrong – commit sin and has caused that child pain for life.

I've told you true love cannot lie or harm but love does because love is a lie. A prime example of this is a man or woman say they love you and cheat on you even abuse you. That is not true love it is love and it is a lie because that person has and have caused you pain. He did you wrong and by so doing made you guilty of sin.

None of you can say I did not teach you about truth and true love. I did so live by it. And no not all parents teach their children these things because they believe and do not know God's ways.

If it is found that the child lied then the lashing is doubled unto that person that lied. If the person cannot handle the lashes then his or her family must stand the penalty and get the lashes in the child's steed.

Lying is a grave sin and I know we do it we are all guilty of sin but in God's world sin is not tolerated and this is why we are changed in the spiritual realm before we move onwards to God's kingdom.

The lashing is harsh but over time this will serve as a deterrent for all including adults.

Secure your children and make sure they are in their homes at an appropriate hour because often times I hear from you "mom some parents don't care what their children do." Do not be like those parents because they are the ones to cry crocodile tears when something goes wrong with their children. They are the ones to swear that their child is good and when the law read out the nature of their children's crime they hold their heads down in shame and say I can't believe my child would do such a thing.

Know your children even better than I know you because I know all of you and what you are all capable of.

If you are selling anything and you know the product have a defect indicate the defect. If the person turn around and sue you for that defect you have proof that you indicated the defect in the contract. A man cannot sue you for the truth he can only sue you for your lies. That which you lied to him about.

Never give up your rights to accept wrong for anyone. I did and it almost cost me my life this is why I am telling you if you are right never ever infinitely never ever abandon your right to accept another man or woman's fault.

Never listen to those that say you have to give up your right just to have peace. Never do it those are the ones that will turn their backs on God to accept the wrong and lies that Evil tells them. Keep your rights.

People will come to you and say your mother is a racist or prejudice but I have not racism or prejudice in my heart. The truth is the truth if I don't like you I don't like you. If I don't want you coming to my door do not come to my door because I don't like you. This is not racism. I refuse to be a hypocrite and parasite.

If a man don't want you in their country do not fight to go there. Do not be eggsup. Say the hell out of his country plain and straight. God has given you a wonderful home and land explore it and spend your money in the lands that God gave to you. The devil's domain is not yours so leave it to the devil.

God and the devil don't mix so don't mix with the devil. If you are with God stay with God. The problem with humanity is if you don't like a person you are a racist. You don't have to like everyone. Do not hate them or wish them harm. Do not do harm to them.

Let's put it this way if I am a racist then God is a racist.

No for real I am not fooling you. Read Psalms 1 of the bible and see how God tells you to live. We are to separate from evil so if by doing this constitute racism and hatred then yes God is a racist a bigot and yes he is infinitely prejudice.

Organic is best so make sure all that you plant is free of chemicals and chemical bi-products.

Never walk in the way of evil

Do not pray like the heathens by bowing down to the dead and say it is God you are praying to. God is not dead he is alive.

If God was dead like I've said all of humanity including the universe would die. They would cease to exist.

Do not go into the churches of heathens to seek God or say you are worshipping God because the heathens pray unto the dead in their worship and praise. They worship and pray the Babylonian way – the deceitful and abominable way. They say they love God and are praying to God but yet disrespect God by trampling God down with their shoes. They desecrate the places meant for the true and living God. In their homes they take off their shoes. They give their homes respect but to God they have no respect because they leave their shoes on and disrespect God in every way.

Never forget to take your shoes off in the house of God because God will hate and despise you for this act.

Always remember a man that say they are in the spirit and speaks in tongues speak only to the devil. They speak the language of the devil because the language of God is never spoken only written by those that God elect – chose.

Do not follow the ways of the Babylonians because they are the ones to cause you and your forefathers to sin. They are the ones to cause you to lose your soul.

Nothing that they do is clean because they are the ones to hate based on colour of skin.

They are the ones to pit nations against nations based on colour of skin.

They are the ones to cause you to worship the dead because their God died long before the conception of man. They know that their God is white a white man in the spiritual realm because evil dies as a white person in the spiritual realm. Know that God is neither white nor is he black he is the energy in the darkness that man and spirit cannot see. When I say spirit cannot see I mean your spiritual eye. If you are confused look at the Ying and the Yang. This I am giving you is the absolute truth and this truth cannot be changed to suit man or any culture. So long as you are evil whether you are White, Indian, Black or Chinese you die as a white person in the spiritual realm. This is how the spirit dies and let no heathen whether Christian, Catholic, Muslim, Protestant or anyone of any religion tell you otherwise. You have the truth and now you know it so keep it and never let it go.

Trust me and infinitely know that the Babylonians know the truth but they alter the truth to save their own knowing full well what they do is wrong and it causes you to sin – die.

Know them meaning know the Babylonians. They are Egyptians, Persians, and Phoenicians. Their original language was and still is Sandscript. Sandcript is the mother tongue for every language on the face of the planet. Know that Urdu comes from Sandscript. Arabic comes from Urdu and if you know about the tower of Babel you now know why they said God separated the languages and cause them to be confused. Know this God did not confuse the heathens as they traveled their dialect changed and this is why there are so many dialects of Urdu which is Arabic.

Know that God has nothing to do with the heathens. They are not God's people.

To the Babylonians you are nothing but lowly slaves

You must be conquered

You must be enslaved

Go back to Genesis where they said God said to have dominion over the fishes of the sea and the animals. Know that God never told us to have dominion over anything. We lived in peace and harmony long ago but because we had compassion for them – we fell inlove with them and despite the warnings from God we did not listen and they enslaved us. They caused us to lose our crown of glory and yes our spirituality.

Know that the Babylonians care not for you but do everything for their own. Their God which is sin and death he is white – evil. Their God is buried under the ground and this is why they have you bowing to the ground.

Remember and never forget that the flesh hath no importance but the spirit/soul is vital to life. It is important. Never forget the more evil have you basking in sin the more life and humanity dies.

Never forget that one sin affects us all because we are all linked in some way no matter how small. And yes that link is God.

Know your colours and know the colours of God because colours are vital in the spiritual world.

Know that everything hath colour and because you cannot see it does not mean it is not there.

Green, Yellow and White are the colours of God.

Black, Blue and White are the colours of evil.

Good and evil wear white but know how pure white is used in the spiritual realm this is vital.

If you know black is a negative colour for you (the colour not the skin tone) meaning if you see someone dressed in black run like there is no tomorrow because that person is not good for you. They do not represent good and God does not want you around that person. Do not go into his abode or realm. Stay permanently away from him or her.

Never forget the colour of skin is vital in the spiritual world but not vital in the physical world and I am going to repeat myself here. When evil dies in the spiritual world they die as a white person. Good cannot die. Good moves on to a higher plain so never hate anyone based on the color of skin this is infinitely wrong because man do not know what lies ahead of them.

Every good person must become black and in the spiritual world and this is why evil tells humanity to hate black people. Every race under the face of the sun hates black people and none know why they are hating them. Do not be like them and never infinitely never hate based on race because all race that is evil must die as white and all race that is good must go on as black. This is how God showed me and this is how I am relating it to you. Never let anyone tell you otherwise.

If you see a ring in the spiritual realm more specifically a gold ring and the angel of God is pointing at a woman or man (one you know in the physical- she could be your boyfriend or girlfriend) do not I repeat do not marry him or her. God is telling you not to marry her. Stay clear from them because they are not clean nor are they holy. Know that God does not use gold. Gold is worthless – garbage in the eyes of God. Gold is thrown away – discarded in the spiritual realm.

Never forget that God's abode do not have gold nor is there any streets of gold there. Gold is worthless to god.

Shiny things – silver those are precious in the sight and eyes of God. Crystals are precious in the eyes of God. God loves silver because silver is one of the makeup of your genes especially your hair. Your hair is your crown of gold – white gold so always keep your hair clean and neat.

In all you do try your best not to add chemicals to it meaning chemically treat it because the angels of God do not wear nor do they have chemically treated hair.

Yes wear your hair long and cut it only if you have committed abominable acts of sin unto God.

By cutting your hair you are repenting meaning you are admitting shame and guilt. Your hair meaning the cutting of your hair is your sin offering meaning your shame and guilt offering unto God. And no it is not a sin to keep your hair neat and clean meaning cut low. Yes women can cut their hair low and wear it low at all times. When I have more information from God when it comes to the hair I will tell you. But always keep your hair neat and clean.

Never ever infinitely never ever bask in blood offerings like the heathens because this is an abomination unto God. It is a sin that is not forgivable.

Your penance for this is your hair. When you have committed abominable acts unto God you must cut your hair. Yes shave your head bald. You must accept guilt – sin once you have done this you will be walking right with God.

Remember women seen their period meaning pass blood every 27-28 days. This is called their monthly cycle and this is because we accepted death. Also know that over time her monthly cycle will change to 36-38 days. I do not know what this change represent but when I do know I will tell you.

Know that God has never ever infinitely never killed anyone because if he did all would die.

Never forget about the Ying and the Yang because this is vital in the spiritual world

Know that good are the ones that are change in the spiritual world but evil cannot change. Evil must and will die. The way you see good changing in the spiritual realm is an operation. As if they are being operated on.

Know infinitely know that evil is female in the physical and spiritual world and this is why evil cannot change. Look at the female genes and know.

Do not hate females because of this because good is female in the physical and male in the spiritual hence God is male in the spiritual and female in the physical.

Male is male but female is both

Like I said do not hate females because of this nor say it is because of them evil came into the world because it is not so. Know the truth. The full truth and how things came into being.

Remember the story of Jesus that is a story Jesus never existed because he cannot be found in the spiritual realm. Yes the story of Jesus is a fraud as it is taken from Babylonian history. Remember the Babylonians practiced incest long before we came out of the land of God. Yes you would have read about the land of Nod. Nod was the land all evil resided in hence good and evil knew about each other.

If you know the story of Jesus remember Nicodemus asked Jesus if a man can go back into his mother's womb once he has been born and Jesus told him he must be born again. This is a lie. Evil cannot be born again evil must die. Before evil dies he must go back to the source – the source of its life which is female. Meaning that which gave it life. Do you hear me? Know this and let no man woman or spirit tell you otherwise. Do not listen to the heathens and say you must be born again because neither good nor evil are born again. Both good and evil must go back to their source and for evil that source is female. Evil must return unto a female at death. This is why evil and the heathens say you must be born again. Evil would like to be born again but it cannot be. Evil must die there is not ands ifs or buts about this. Evil will and must die.

Now you comprehend, overstand and understand why males beat females and but them down but don't you do it. Females are good and evil. God will show you the good ones.

Respect females because we are the carrier of life whether good or bad.

Know infinitely know that the father son and holy ghost analogy represents 3 (three) females in the spiritual realm. Trust me these females are beautiful and young. Each have the mark of the beast as man calls it. Each one have 666 on their forehead but do not count the father of sin out. He also have 6 (six) thousand years thus the cycle of evil is 24000 years hence man uses a 24 hour clock to represent a day.

Some say good have 12 hours and bad have 12 hours but do not listen to them nor listen to the 24 elder analogy of their being 12 good elders and 12 bad elders this is infinitely wrong and false. Bad meaning evil hath 24000 years or a day to do all the evil it can do.

For good time is infinite because good cannot die but evil can and do die.

Know that man do not die right away. Meaning death is scheduled long before a person dies when he or she dies is his time meaning physical time has caught up to spiritual time. The correct time. And no a baby don't just die like that his time was scheduled too.

Know that evil can take a life from the spiritual world. Man calls this crib death because they know not of the wicked and evil spirits that lurks in the dark and this is why I tell you to dedicate your children unto the good service of God and ask God to protect and shield your child at all times from the touch and breathe of evil. Like I've told you evil cannot go where it is not wanted meaning if you do not let evil in evil cannot come in. Evil have to be invited in.

Know that evil walk amongst man and those that can see them can hear them and talk to them.

Know that evil does all to kills because it must kill. Evil must shed blood.

Remember there is no remission of sin for the shedding of blood because you are taking a life. Yes the spirit lives on but you are killing the body – the flesh.

Yes the spirit seeks to escape the body meaning the flesh because the flesh is its prison. The body is a jailhouse for the spirit but it does not mean another should kill it – take the life from it.

Do not let anyone put you in debt like I have said because many debts cannot be repaid.

Do not live to put yourself in debt because debts are hard to come out of and it is a sin.

Our forefathers put us in debt and look at the debt can we repay it without having to have to die and even when we die we cannot repay it because many of us go straight to hell and die
If you are leader of a country meaning the people elect you leader do not put your country in debt because of your people. Know that they will cause you to run your country to a muck then turn around and blame you.

Run your country honest and clean. Do not buy what you cannot afford because of your people.

Never infinitely never fight another man's or country's war for them because they are the ones to turn around and hate you and yes they are the ones to bankrupt you

Think of your country's future. If your subjects are people are willing to sacrifice their country meaning want your country to be in debt because of them walk away meaning resign your post as leader and let them elect someone else that will give them all that they want. Do you hear me let them elect someone else to put them in debt because none of them are thinking about tomorrow – their future and their off springs future. They are the ones to put themselves in debt because of their own greed then turn around and cry to God for help. Yes they even blame God and they knew what they are doing is wrong.

Hear me and walk away from them let them feel the pains of their sorrows and if they elect you to come back and help do not return because they were against you and more importantly they were against God. They stood against God. Do not think I have not had arguments about God for this. I have told him to leave humanity alone because time and time again we have chosen evil above him. We do not care about him so leave us alone and let evil do to us at will. None of us meaning no one can blame God for this because he did send us help time and time again and we refused to listen.

If a man do not want you in their land or apart of his group or company do not sue him nor call him racist. Leave him the hell alone.

Do not infinitely never ever fight a man for his own. This is his and you have no right to sue him or her for it. This is wrong.

Do not meaning never ever fight to lay with evil or go into his or her abode. Leave evil alone evil is not your right. Get your own and have your own. As blacks some of us are too damned licky licky and red eyed. Know these people and stay away from them because they are the ones that will kill you for your own.

Never say a man is racist because he does not want you to be apart of his group. He's not racist he just does not want you there. If he excludes all blacks based on race still leave him alone. KNOW THE SAYING AND ADHERE TO IT. WHERE NO DOGS ARE ALLOWED NO BONES ARE PROVIDED. Leave him alone. You have the say meaning you have control over your life. Do not go into his store and buy his product. Do not watch his television programs, do not buy his clothes, do not buy his food. Do not convene with him. Know the clean black stores and shop there. Lift up your own. Do not do this based on the colour of skin but based on the goodness and cleanliness of the person because you all know that good is black and evil is white meaning every person that do good is black and every person that practice and do evil is white. So not all blacks are blacks some are white based on the evil that they do and accept.

Know the truth of God at all times and keep this truth dear and near to you.

Know the truth of Adam and Eve

Know the truth of Moses

Know the truth of you and all that you do

Know infinitely know that everyone hath a tree of life so know your tree of life. Mine is a tomato tree – plant, yours could be a guava tree, a jackfruit tree, a almond tree so know yours because God will use it to show you how your life will be with that person. Eve's tree of life was the apple tree and trust me we all eat from this tree when we do something wrong. Meaning if God is showing you a person and telling you not to be with them he will use your tree of life to show you your future with the person. This we need to comprehend. It does not necessarily mean the person is evil it just mean that he or she is not the right one for you. You will be stressed and your life will not be happy with this person. He or she is wrong for you.

Yes if the person is evil trust me God will show you them descending on you in a full suit of black and this means he is spiritual and physically evil. Stay away from him or her because this person is sent to kill you – take your life so know your colors and stay true to the colors God have given to you and shown you. Never deviate from them because the day you do you will surely die.

Know the scent of evil spirits. Do you hear me know the scent of evil spirits and let no one tell you you cannot smell evil or know when a person is going to die.

You can tell when a person is going to die and you can smell evil. Evil – the scent of evil smells like shit – pooh. Its stinks like hell worse than hell. This is the scent of evil. Sometimes you will smell the scent of musk and jasmine these are good spirits passing through. They cannot stay nor can they linger they are on their way.

Some people at times see a glow around the person when they are going to die but know that it is not all that can see this glow.

I cannot see this glow but can tell you when someone is going to die meaning you see death before you months before the person dies. Sometimes this gets scary because the faces are mangled meaning that person is going to die a horrible death yes in a disaster. You see faces that you do not know and do not know what to make of it. Disasters I have seen but it is not clear meaning with me I have to decipher many things and many times I cannot I can only wait until the dream/vision comes to pass. And yes this is where lies come in meaning some of us decipher wrong.

Sometimes I wish I had someone that could help me decipher them but because I don't I leave many things alone.

Know the distance between God and man because trust me the distance is very far and no the distance cannot be measured by a mere man. The number must be given unto you

Know that God will give you and show you many things but it is up to you not to be lazy.

Know evil must kill everything that is good but the one thing that evil fail to realize is that no matter what he or she does to flesh they cannot do to spirit because evil hath no authority over the spirit. The only way evil has authority over the spirit is if we sell our souls to evil and yes if we accept evil in all that we do.

Remember God cannot go against the Ying and the Yang for man or spirit everything must live according to this.

Know that time cannot change to please anyone or anything. Time is constant it is just man that lags behind in time.

Know that man say everything is measured in waves - wavelengths but man cannot measure wavelengths because he knows not the wavelengths in time meaning the distance of each wavelength in time.

Know that light in its original state cannot bend it is straight. Man cannot see the light of God so how can he say light bends when he cannot see true light nor smell light.

Yes man say they can travel at the speed of light but man cannot travel at the speed of light. If they could they would be able to reach and see God in his purest of forms. Man travels at the speed their body can accommodate meaning the speed at which their body can tolerate before their organs – flesh shuts down. Man hath not the technology to determine the true speed of light.

Know the significance and importance of water and always keep the waterways clean and pure

Look up do you see the blue sky know that this blue energy is power and it does affect life on all levels meaning it hinders life and this is why it is said as it is above so it is below and yes this is the cause for the deciphering of dreams because truth have to go through this negative field.

Do not hate evil or evil people because when you do you are giving into them – giving into their negativity and yes this will cause you to hate them

Never let no one tell you that the devil was in heaven with God because where God resides no evil is there and can never enter there.

Remember the heathens tell you that Satan was a beautiful singer. That is an infinite lie this is his name. His name is Singh – Sing – Singer. Let no one tell you otherwise because their book of lies do tell you ¼ of the truth so know the truth and adhere to the words of God.

Like I said do not hate evil and wicked people and let no one tell you that black people did not reside in the land of Babylon because we did. Every land across the globe blacks resided and still reside.

Remember evil hath no claim to earth nor does he have a claim to God's kingdom.

Remember what I said if you do not allow evil in evil cannot come in. Once you give evil permission to come in they will take all from you by any means necessary. No it did not have to be this way but evil wanted it this way hence evil dies and must die but life lives on forever. Life cannot die because it is truth everlasting and that truth is God.

Never say an evil people cannot get into God's abode. God does not shut anyone out. All can get in including wicked and evil people but they must repent and live a clean and good life. They cannot hate based on skin colour. They cannot live a life of sin they must live a life of truth.

Yes certain sins are not forgiven and they are automatic death. You know those because they are mentioned above.

Know infinitely know that God will never tell you to rape rob and steal from anyone

Know infinitely know that God will never tell you to kill

Yes we eat the carcass of the dead because not everyone can eat vegetables and for this God will not skin you. Meaning God does not sin you if you killed an animal to eat food. Yes it did say God gave us all the herb yielding trees to eat of but it is not all vegetables or herbs that are good to consume and this goes for animals as well.

Know the foods that are clean to eat

Try your best not to consume more than your belly can tolerate

Know that genetics does not determine the weight of a person it is what we consume. Know that many foods are made to make you obese because many foods are genetically modified to kill man over time.

Know your limits and respect yourself. If you cannot respect yourself you cannot respect God nor can you do right by God.

In all that you do meaning if God gives you a farm make the food that you grow be respectable in the sight of God meaning make your food organic. Never add chemicals to kill yourself or man. Meaning never use chemicals to kill any form of life. Preserve the culture and the way of life God has given to you and never deviate from this to suit or please the greed of man and yes your family.

Stretch a helping hand to the poor and your family if you can because it is a foolish man that stores up his riches and loses his soul in the end.

Give what you can give never what you can't and absolutely never give to get in return. Give with a clean and pure heart.

Yes you must save what you can for old age. Enjoy your old age because when you are gone you cannot enjoy that which you have saved on earth. Someone else will come and enjoy it and trust me you will cry in the grave.

Store up your wealth and goodness in God meaning all the good that you do store it up in God because it is needed after death. This is your happiness in the afterlife. Trust me you will do the tatty and moonwalk in happiness unto God. Trust me you will shout and sing thank you God I have made it. On earth we don't think of this but you need to think of where you are going to go in the hereafter because life does not stop it continues unto God.

Like I've said you do not have to worry about where you go if you do good in the sight of God. God cannot refuse you from his abode when you do good. Goodness moves on to a happier and better life but evil cannot move on it dies

If you are married to a Babylonian do not say oh my god God does not like me and I am going to go to hell. Do not be like the heathens that will now do this. When you do this you would have sinned and you are sinning because of this. You would not be true to your mate. I told you God does not sin you for the truth he cannot. If you and her or him are living a truthful and clean life meaning you do not indulge in sin, you do not practice idol worship, witchcraft, human and animal sacrifices all that is evil in the sight of God then you do not have to worry about it. Know what I said. It is the sins that we do that prevents us from living a clean and pure life. We follow and bask in sin and kill ourselves. We all have the gene(s) of sin in us and this is why I tell you to plead with God to take it from you and never let your children and grand children be born with the gene (s) of sin. Pray to God meaning tell him what you need and want in a good way and he will grant you this. Before you have children plead with God and ask him to take the genes of sin from your children and any future generation that will come from your loins and the loins of your children – your bloodline. None must be born with the sinful genes. Please do this for me and God and live. Live a clean and good life because God is clean and good.

We as humans are the ones to be unclean.

We are the ones to put God to shame and disgrace in all that we do.

We are the ones to let God hold his head down and cry so always be truthful to God.

Live and walk in your integrity which is God's integrity. I have sinned big time against God but now I know the truth of him therefore I do my best to do better and not walk in the way of sin.

Live by your truth and the truth of God. Remember no man can correct his wrongs but we all can change our future.

The truth is the truth. You must live in truth. Yes the Babylonians are wicked and evil but God did not shut them out of his abode. God shut their evils out of his abode and because they bask in sin meaning their evils they cannot get into God's abode.

No sin can enter into God's abode and this is why the spirit is changed in the spiritual realm. You see this as an operation a medical procedure that has to do with the head. The head is significant in the spiritual realm.

So because of sin do not marry a Babylonian nothing else. They were the ones to lie to Eve and that lie stuck unto this day. I am going to be racist here but when I was growing up it was said when a coolie tell a lie on you that lie stick. It stick for life and you cannot get rid of it. This is like the lie Satan told to Eve and that lie has stuck from generation unto generation and none of us can get rid of it. We don't want to get rid of it we want to walk and bask in sin.

Know that when Satan told Eve she would not die he Satan was saying God is a liar. He God was not telling her the truth. Eve did die. She died spiritually and physically.

She was the one to open the door to evil because she did have children with Satan. Know who they are because they too spread their lies and call it Islam.

Follow no form of religion because God never infinitely never gave religion unto man to worship or praise him.

Give God thanks at all times because God is life and he more than deserves our love.

Grow up your children in the truth of God and teach them to respect themselves. Teach them to respect their culture and heritage. Teach them to never stray from their heritage nor accept another man's heritage and call it their own.

If you or your off springs marries another from another race say A Russian or Scott respect his or her heritage but do not walk in the ways of their sins. Respect the language and heritage but the sins of man do not bask in it. Learn the language and teach your children the language because this is your heritage.

Disrespect no one. This will seem confusing but trust God to teach you were I have failed because I know what I mean but the language barrier to explain what I mean is not clear.

Teach your children and tell them no one can be converted because God converts no one. Evil converts but God never converts.

Teach them and tell them no one can die for their sins. Your sins are your own and you must give an account for them in the grave.

Know that if evil wants into God's abode they must come clean and stop the hatred because they are the ones to hate God and do all in their power to kill God and his good people.

Know that the heathen will come to you with everything but know them they are the ones that say God we love you but yet do what they are not to do. Remember the song Moses Moses take off thy shoes because the place you are standing on is holy ground. Moses took off his shoes and respected God but the heathens disrespect God at all times because they do not take their shoes off on God's holy ground.

Know infinitely know this is why God hates the Ethiopians because they disgraced God by walking in his holy temples with their shoes. If God hates the Ethiopians for this what say you?

Do not be like the careless Ethiopians because they did mix their seeds with the Babylonians therefore they were conquered and their land became desolate and unholy.

Let no one tell you that Moses parted the Red Sea because Moses did not part the Red Sea it was parted long before Moses. This you know because the Ethiopians had the keys to the elements. They were the ones that were in control of the weather. Lightning and thunder they could produce at will and because they disgraced God the key was taken from them.

Know that God did not send Moses into Ethiopia if Moses had journeyed into Ethiopia then yes we could say without a shadow of a doubt that Moses parted the Red Sea because he would have gotten the key from the Ethiopians. Moses did not journey their nor did he have the keys to the elements – weather. Let no one tell you otherwise because evil lies and cannot deviate from his lies.

Know infinitely know that evil lies. This is what it did to God. Evil lied about God and like I said we are following this lie unto this day. We refuse the seek the truth of God.

Know this if the Babylonians rise again then all humanity will be destroyed like I've said because many of you will be jobless

Many will go without food

This time around your slavery will be worse because you will have to kiss evil's ass because there will be one world order, one religion, one god that you will have to bow down to, one currency, one everything because death will reign supreme.

No one can blame God for this because this is what we chose and choose.

Never forget the flood of Noah because the flood was contained to one land. It was not global like man would have you believe.

Learn and listen our ancestors did not listen and an entire race was almost wiped out except for Noah and his family. Do not be like our ancestors of the past and walk unto their death. Remember when God closed the door of the Ark no one could get in. They perished. Noah and his family stayed on the track of God even though people laughed at him. He never strayed because he listen and he was saved. The rest of his people died because they did not trust God nor did they know God. When it was too late was when they were knocking down God's door and God did not open it. God took who trusted him and listened to him to safety.

Never ever be like our ancestors of old in their wicked and evil ways.

God has and have given us people to teach us and tell us the truth we are the ones to toss and throw them aside for evil and when it's too late for us we say we are repenting. Don't make it be too late for you.

Never forget that Eve chose her faith and she did die.

The people of Noah's time chose their faith and they did die

Solomon did chose his faith and he lost it all and did die

Jesus if you look at it from a story standpoint but know that he did not exist but for those that believe that he did he too died. He made people believe he was the son of God and he did die but God did not take humanity with him. Humanity lived so humanity was speared but this humanity does not know.

God will never commission nor will God lead or send his people unto death. God would never ever do this so stay firm to God and walk with him at all times meaning keep God in your thoughts at all times.

Remember King David did kill and he did not reach the highest plain of God. Blood was on his hands so never indulge in blood.

Remember the 24 hour clock as noted above. Know that evil works 24 hours per day. Evil never stops and this is why 24 is significant to evil.

Respect God and your body do not follow the heathens and desecrate the temple God has given you.

None of God's angel's have body art so get none. Respect yourself.

Know that the world and every race including your own hates you because of your colour but respect it because God is black hence he would not make us in his image which is the image of darkness black. This may sound racist to you and others but it was not meant to be just look at the hue of the darkness the night. Do not look at it in a physical context but a spiritual one.

Never forget to life for life and teach your children this because the day you live for death you will die

Infinitely never ever let anyone tell you that God is dead. Are you not alive so how can God be dead?

Think and let God open up is kingdom to you at all time.

God is the key and he is your keep so stay with him no matter what the heathens do to you. Remember I did make God my friend and I take everything out on him but the day he leaves me I will die so I cannot leave him. I have to stay with him.

Listen respect is key and like I've said if you cannot respect yourself you cannot respect God and trust me no one will respect you.

Life is the key to our existence and let no one take that from you not even evil. Guard your life it is yours to keep. Evil have no right to lie to anyone to take their life. It is wrong and evil is wrong. Evil cannot and will never get right for the wrongs he has done so do not under any circumstances follow evil nor follow evil and wicked people.

The heathens will tell you you can find God in churches but do not follow them because God is not sinful or dirty so stay away and out of the domain and places of the wicked and sinful. They do not have the love of God. They defile and disrespect God at all time.

They go as far as speaking for God when God did not tell them to speak on his behalf.

Never ever forget that God has a voice and he can speak for himself. God chose no man to speak for him not even me. So when a man or woman say they are speaking for God as well as acting on the behalf of God run them meaning walk away from them in this sense because God chose none of us to act on his behalf nor speak for him because none of can represent God. We are all dirty in some way. Yes we try to be clean but our past sins made us dirty and none of us can clean up our sins without the grace and mercy of God so do no sin nor bask in it.

Do not follow the heathens and have many wives because this is an abomination unto God. It causes strife and it does cause hate. The act of having more than one wife is whoredom. It is a sin because a man cannot love one without hating another. The art of marrying more than one wife is of man and not of God because God does not like whoredom.

The male giveth life and the female receiveth life so respect life

Do not follow the heathens and mutilate the female genitalia this is a grave sin and injustice unto life. This is not of God but of man. Woe be unto the man that does this because they are mutilating God because God is female in the physical and male in the spiritual. This is a great disrespect and dishonor unto God who is male and female.

Never commit adultery because this is an abomination in the sight of God. You must never have wife or girlfriend at home and have a sweetheart down the road this is wrong. If you have one mate at home keep that one mate.

Always give your body time and space if you have broken up with someone. Do not do like the heathens and get involved right away when they have left someone.

Know that these things my mother and grandmother did not teach me. These things my mother did not know so I am teaching them to you.

Never forget that divorces are there. If you divorce by man standards divorce by God's standards as well meaning when man divorce you seek a divorce from your wife or husband from God. This is where the wedding band comes into play because that band is discarded by God and you are divorced from the person you ask God for a divorce from. This I know because I did ask God to divorce me from all the men I have been with and the divorce was granted unto me. This is why I tell you that gold is discarded in the spiritual realm it has no value.

Never be like the heathens because many have committed adultery in the eyes of God because none seeks a divorce from him when they divorce man.

In order to divorce from man go to God truthfully and tell him in this manner. God I come before you with truth. I have been before man and sort a divorce between me and my wife (name of wife) and it has been granted now I am coming before you and asking you to grant me a divorce. Please accept my petition and divorce me (your name and her name) from your record books. God we are no longer man and wife but we have gone our separate ways and it is in good faith that I come to you to grant me this divorce so that I do not sin if I take another wife or mate. (your name). This is the like manner that you must pray in and no not on your knees sit in your sofa, lay upward on your bed, sit around the dinner table. Where ever you have deemed holy to speak to God speak to him and be truthful. You can tell God the problems you had with your wife. Let God be your confession not man meaning talk to him about everything and don't be ashamed. Talk to him about sex too if you have sexual issues and he will show you what to do.

Never forget that God can and will answer you in the form of a song, a television program, a movie, a strangers smile, a phone call.

Never forget too that if God wants and need you to learn a lesion he will put you in the place you need to learn the lesson. I know this first hand. Trust me on this because God showed me firsthand how perfect and true a lie can seem. I am a living testament of this and this is why I tell all of you to be truthful at all times no matter the consequence. Lie for no one because that lie reflect on God and it does hurt him. This I know.

Never give evil the edge over God. I did and trust me it does not make me feel good inside but now that I know the truth I tell

God to wipe lying from my lips and never let me bask in it.

Lies are hurtful and it is painful I know. In all that I do God knows me and know my truth and yes I have told him if he ever make me lie to the people of this world in my books he had better shut me out of his abode because I will make his life a living nightmare yes hell. All of you have seen what I have been through at the hands of evil and wicked people and I refuse to be like the heathens – wicked and evil people. No life is life and everyone has a right to life and no one have a right to take your life not even evil.

Evil have not right but yet he deceives and kill anyway and this is why I say and tell you stay away from evil. Do not go into the lands of wicked and evil people. This is not godly. Evil has his domain and he does not have a right to come into your domain and destroy it. It is not right.

If a man don't want you in his country do not be like some blacks and force to go. Stay the hell out. That's there domain. Be happy and thankful with the domain God has given unto you. Respect the land, beautify it and live clean. Respect yourself and your country.

Know that it is not all countries that are good for you. Build up your country in the name of God. Bring God the true and living God into your country and trust me infinitely you will succeed. You will prosper because your country will now have true life and that is the life of God.

Remember the cunning ways of evil because it is a foolish man that builds up and stores up weapons and neglect their economy. Never forget about your economy because evil does not forget about it. The economic forefront is his goal and weapon also so never ever infinitely never ever forget about your economy.

Remember evil will have you fighting a losing battle because no one can win evil on the battleground or battlefield. This is evils domain. He is the master of it but you can win and defeat him on the economic forefront by not putting yourself or your country in debt for him.

Look at the economy today and learn from each countries mistakes by never forgetting the lie that evil told Eve. She accepted his evil and everyone in the garden became tainted. One sin does pollute all that is good so be careful who you lay with, befriend and do business with.

Never forget the book of lies because it did state that we are a bunch of stiff necked people that do not listen. This is not wrong it is the truth because we die for evil. Give our lives to evil. We have children with evil and yes we dedicate our children to evil and when God sends his messengers to bring us back on the right track we fight against them even kill them and say they are the evil ones. Know the messengers that God have given to you. Know God and never believe because belief fades, converts and conquer but knowing – knowledge can never fade, convert or be conquered. Your knowledge is solid and it can never change.

Remember the devil uses his analogy to catch you by saying ¼ + ¼ + ¼ + ¼ = 1 but it cannot equal one it can only equal 4. Just count how many quarters you have so how can it equal one? If you put them together or divide you get one they say but you cannot get one you will still have 4. There is no division when it comes to God because division is a lie. It is an absolute lie and can never be true because God divides nothing. The devil or evil divides but God separates and never divides. Remember the saying a country divided will fall. This is infinitely true so never divide the truth but separate the lies meaning separate good from evil and live in unity with God. When you do this you can never fall.

When you have children be there for them and never abandon them like some men do. They have children here there and everywhere and neglect them. Never neglect your children. Support them and be there for them no matter what.

Raise your children in the right manner like I've said and they will honor you and make you proud.

Never let a woman have to take you before the law for child support. Your children or child is your responsibility and it is your right to look after them by providing for them because no child asked to come into this world. You and your mate fathered them out of pleasure so do all that is right and just by them.

If you are not working and she is your duty is to babysit them.
If you are in jail your duty is to call them and make sure homework is done and they are doing well in school. Not because you are incarcerated means your duty as a father stops it does not because you too can help them with their homework and tell them as well as teach them not to follow in your pathway of sin and evil. You can make sure that they do right. Turn your negative into a positive and make sure your child's mother keep you updated on your child. You have family members let family members keep a tab on them because many times you hear if daddy was there I would have turned out

better so do not be like the worthless fathers of this world be there for your children because it was not the mother alone that conceived the child you played a part in the role.

If you are a part of your child's life never let a stepfather punish your child you scold them. This is your child and your duty as a father is to scold them when they are wrong and never ever infinitely never ever turn your child against his or her stepfather because he is providing for your child so thank him every now and then and respect him because he is helping you to raise your child.

Never ever use your children or child as a pawn in any custody battles. It is a worthless man and woman uses their children as pawns in their custody games. I repeat it is a worthless man and woman that uses their child or children as pawns in their custody games.

Have joint custody of your children meaning both of you share duties. If you think it wise for the child or children to stay with mom and go to school then agree on it and do all you can to help the money pay any school fees, daycare cost, living expenses that will be incurred and never abandon your child if she is being a bitch because some women are bitches they care not for the child only the money.

Never ever infinitely never ever pay a woman cash for child support. Use cheques, money orders or direct deposit. If you use direct deposit let it specify child support payment with the transit number. Keep an accurate record and never falsify documents to say you have paid money when you have not. It is a worthless and deceiving man or woman that does so.

The reason why I tell you this is because some woman will take you to court and say you did not pay them anything and you will not have a record to say that you did so be wise because many women are deceitful and cunning.

Make sure that you are at every parent teacher interview with your child no matter if you and her are not together. This is your right and you must know how your child is doing in school in order to help them.

Reward your child for good behavior but not all the time or they will expect it all the time.

If they get good grades tell them you are proud of them and at the end of the school year take them out with their friends if you can do so.

Sometimes take your child to lunch. Pop up at their schools and take them to lunch and let them feel good.

Never forget children hold their fathers in high esteem and when daddy is gone they do feel abandoned so always be there for them and never steer them wrong because they will hold you accountable. They will hold you wrong so teach them right at all times.

Teach them to be open and honest with you at all times just as I have done to all of you.

Always be open and honest with them just as I have done with all of you.

Never love one more than the other because if you did your love would not be true. You can do more for one than the other but this is based on deeds not true love. Meaning if you tell your child to do his chores and he refuses to do it or put it off do more for the one that do their chore and if the one that did not do their chore gets mad ask him or her why they are mad and tell them the reason why you did what you did. They did not do their chores hence they could not enjoy in the fun.

Never tell a child "you know what you did that's why you are being punished" that is wrong.

If you scold your child by spanking him or her ask them if they know why they are being scolded. If they say they do not know tell them it was because they stole a chain if they stole a chain and stealing is wrong. If they were fighting tell them it was because they were fighting and fighting is wrong.

Never infinitely never ever give your child right when you know they are wrong. This I have learnt so I no longer do this.

Never sell a man broken goods and say it is good if you do you are wrong and do not blame the man if he sues you for all you have because you knew what you did was wrong and sinful.

If your product is broken say it is broken and if he or she still wants it then sell it to him or her he cannot come back to you and say you sold him defective product because he knew going into the contract that the product was defective so therefore he cannot sue you.

Never take your friends goods and sell it for them because if anything goes wrong the person will return to you because you sold him the goods and not your friends and this is why I say do not go into debt for your friends meaning put yourself in trouble for your friends because in the end they are not there for you.

Know that a good and true friend do not let you put yourself in trouble for them.

Know who you co-sign for because many will leave you holding the bag without thought of you. Hence know your friends and how truthful they are. Try your best never to co-sign for anyone because it's a foolish man that takes up responsibilities that he or she cannot handle.

Meaning if he cannot handle his payments now how will he be able to handle his payments in the future. Think

Guard your credit and let no one use it falsely because it's a good man that thinks of it and do all to protect it.
Never forget that there are evil people out there that do not care about you they will take your credit and put you in debt while they have not a care in the world and it is my hope that God turn back the hands of time on all of them because what they are doing is wrong.

Never infinitely never ever rob or steal from the old no matter how evil they are. Never steal period.

Protect the old because in life we grow and we do get old and feeble. No one thinks of the old. No one thinks that they too are going to get old and feeble one day so respect the old and take good council from them because they are very wise in their old age.

Always do good unto the old and trust me God will infinitely bless you because just as you need love the old need love too.

There are many things I do not know but I am trusting God to teach all of you the right and just way.

Many things I do not know but as you get old you will learn and know so that you can teach your children right the just and true way.

Adhere to my teachings because all of you know that God rarely speaks but his language is written meaning his words are written and never spoken.

Truly love silence and the dark because everything is made from light and there is light in the darkness it's man that cannot see the light in the darkness nor can he comprehend it.

Truly love life and you do everything in the universe will be open unto you. You will see greater life in its purity.

Know the Ying and the Yang and whatever you do do good business with the Chinese because they did keep the Ying and the Yang true to God. Never deal falsely with them or dishonor them. Yes some may hate you but never hate them because they are on the first level of God's mountain and I would rather you marry into their fold than marry a Babylonian.

Know that the gifts of God in the spiritual realm is given to them to give unto you. They are a symbol of prosperity in the spiritual realm.

Know symbolism in the spiritual realm because dogs in the spiritual realm represent man. White represents a white male in the physical. Brown represents a black male in the physical but I have yet to find out what an angry black dog in the spiritual represent. When I find out I will let you know.

Cats in the spiritual realm represent evil. Know this that cats will not protect you from evil they will allow evil to conquer and consume you so be careful of them. Yes they are cuddly but they are not devoted to you.

If you have a dog teach him or her well and they will love and protect you.

I am just learning about the bear and its love and devotion to the ones they love. The bear in the spiritual realm also represent man but I am learning about the bear I do not have full comprehension of the bear as yet but what I see they are extremely devoted to the ones they truly love and care about.

There is a winged horse that is black and beautiful like a stallion. The Greeks calls this horse Pegasus and this horse represents a fallen nation. This was long ago before the deep blue sea. Meaning long before we saw the sea as blue the reflection on the water was green and animals were not as small as they are today they were fairly larger – bigger. This is how it was shown to me and this is how I am relating it to you.

Never forget in all that you do know and not believe.

Convert to nothing

Convert to no religion because I did tell you above God converts no one. Evil converts good to evil and evil does use religion and the church to convert you to sin.

God converts no one nor does he change anyone so if a man tells you God will change you run because you know he or she is a liar. You know God cannot go against the Ying and the Yang because all life came about through this meaning the Ying and the Yang.

Know light and that light is different. I cannot tell you about the light because all that I need to know about the light have not been revealed to me so therefore I cannot tell you about it. Hopefully when the clean one comes she will tell you more about the light and how to see the true light of God within you.

Know that your own people will stand against you in hard times but never give up on God he will carry you through.

Always infinitely always be a the root of God and never be branches or leafs but always be the root. Let God be your root as well as grow in the good and true roots of God.

Remember and infinitely never forget anyone can say they love but not many can say they truly love.

Love truthful and God will shine his light through you.

Never ever look at facial beauty because beauty lies within and permeates outwards.

Remember it is a foolish man that bases love on outer beauty and loses his soul

Never ever infinitely never ever pay anyone to be in your company to rub your back and say you make them happy. This is nastiness and whoredom and it make the person no less than a prostitute. Never let anyone be a prostitute for you because you are living a deadly lie and you are letting that person lie for you.

Yes we do things to make ourselves and each other happy but true happiness lies within, In life and even in true love we have pitfalls ups and downs so lie for no one and say you are happy when you are truly unhappy.

Yes I have a truthful relationship with God and God will tell you that I argue with him because I get unhappy with him because at times I am lonely and need him and he is not always there.

Trust your instincts meaning at times you will want to go to a place and your car breaks down for no reason do not go to that place this is God's way of warning you so listen to God. Never go. This has happened to me and I did not listen and trust me I lived to regret not listening so listen to what God is trying to tell you as well as is telling you.

Now be good and always be good so that God can and will find good favor in you.

Let no one tell you that Eve was the mother of civilization because she was not. Life and civilization existed long before Eve.

Let no one tell you that the black race is cursed because we are not and never will be. We the black race turned from God and accepted lies by whoring – laying with sin. Meaning Eve had sex with a sinful man. A man that God told her not to lay with and that is how we fell from grace. We gave up knowledge and a pure way of life for death – sin.

Know that the white race do not know their history because if they did they would not hate black people nor would they buy into the white superiority bullshit that they and the Babylonians spread.

Whites were enslaved. They were fighters and warriors. They were the ones to be deceived not the blacks. Remember we whored. They the whites were the ones to have a spell cast on them. Their own deceived them – sold them out and if they knew their history they would know that the spell of Leviathan as some people call it was cast on them. If they knew their history they would know this. This is how it was shown to me and this is how I am relaying it back to you.

Never forget there is good and bad in every race and none is superior to the other. Good belongs to God and bad belongs to man and evil never forget this.

No one on the face of this planet can say they truly love God and hate their fellow man.

Like I've said every race hate the black race based on color of skin but yet if they read their book of sin they would know that they are bowing down to and paying homage to a black man.

No one can say they hate the black race because if they do they hate God and his angels because they are black.
Be proud of who you are no matter your skin tone – hue because God is proud of you. Damned proud because he made you black and beautiful like him (and this is based on your goodness not colour of skin) because all good is black in the spiritual realm and all evil is white and must die as white – a white person in the spiritual realm. This is how it was shown to me and this is how I am relaying it to you.

Know that the colour of skin is significant in death because this is how evil dies. All that is evil must die as white a white person and this is what humanity and the church fail to teach you. Instead of telling you the truth they tell you lies and send your soul to hell. They sell your soul to evil and then turn around and tell you that you are doing good. Tell me my children how can you be doing good when you are going to die?

No one that hates can enter into God's abode and this goes for me too. If I hate I cannot get in nor can I truly see or love God. I would be wrong and yes I would be sinful. I would be a liar and yes I would be representing God falsely.

Know that the original pharaoh of Egypt is not dead. He was the keeper of the books and trust me there are many books of God but one specific book. One main one that which is called Holy Bible not to be confused with man's holy book which they call the holy bible.

God's book is small very small. I know the colour of it and I will show you one day if you ask.

Know that I cannot teach you how to write the language of God because I cannot write it. Meaning God has not ordained me or told me I can write it. When he gives me permission I will show you if it is God's will and he gives me permission to do so but know I will not be able to teach you to write it.

God's writing is sacred and like I've said only a few know to write it but the one that is chosen to use it can heal anyone at any given time no matter where they are on the planet. This language drives away evil and can keep it at bay – trap it. This is the key that evil is looking for but will never obtain it because they have to be chosen by God and God alone and trust me God does not infinitely not chose an evil person to do his will.

Let no one tell you it is a sin to have an image meaning picture

If you can draw draw your children – take pictures. Evil men and women will tell you not to do so because God said not to have any image in his likeness yahda yahda yahda but don't listen to them. God gave you the art of artistry use that gift truthfully and draw your pictures true to life. Draw everything in its original likeness and do not deviate from the truth to please no one.

Evil and wicked men tell you not to do so because they are the ones to steal your history and say it is theirs – their own. When you do not have a picture of yourself and your ancestors as well as when you do not have a record of your history anyone can substitute theirs for yours and tell you it is your history. They will tell you the land was originally their land and they will do all to take it from you without merit. This is what they did in Egypt. The Babylonians stole our history and books – books they could not interpret they burned. They had to enslave us and gain our knowledge and when they did this they incorporated their history into ours and called it their own. This is why the bible that humanity reads is based on Black and Hindu history. None of it is white history because they could not steal the history of the whites. They eliminated it all together. They knew both races Blacks and Whites were one because they did live in unity and peace long before Eve did what she did. Look at the Ying and Yang for full comprehension if you do not understand what I am saying to you. Now in our day and time if you ask an Egyptian if blacks resided in Egypt some say no and some quinge at the thought of you asking that question. Also this is why they the Egyptians go to every length to eliminate blacks from the history books but it does not matter what they do because our history reside in us. We have records to prove otherwise because the triangle represent us the black race. The ones that God chose are sealed with the upright triangle. Yes it is embedded in our skin and yes this is why the Rastas point the triangle upwards to donate respect of life – growth.

The triangle is a part of life and yes it is also a secret order that was before man. Do not confuse this symbol with the trinity nor confuse it with the orders of evil societies of this day and time because they know not the powers of this order. Those that are under the order of the triangle are special people that are chosen by God to carry on his bloodline meaning they teach you the truth. They also have the key to death and hell meaning they can contain and destroy evil. They have to power to do so because they have true life meaning they live and do things according to the truth that God has given to them and they cannot break the code because it is that sacred.

I will remind you now and yet again all that is good is black. The problem with humanity is that they cannot see beyond black and white. They cannot comprehend the Ying and the Yang.

Know your history like I've said because neither the white race nor the black race and I am now talking about color in the physical context – on a human level. Neither race know their history and this is why both races are being lead astray. We hate each other based on colour of skin but neither know that we need each other.

When you eliminate all the blacks from this planet they are next and the Babylonians will not hesitate to use them at will. They too will have to kiss the Babylonians ass because they did accept their gods and sins.
Do not hate evil and yes wicked and evil people will try to hurt you but if you do not go into their path they cannot hurt you. Some will try based on greed and jealousy but will never hurt you if you are under the protection of God.

Remember I've said and I did not tell you but I am telling you now the two truest books or psalms of the bible are Psalms 1 (one) and Psalms 23 (twenty three).

Psalms 23 is no longer effective because of the sins of man meaning our sins have reached too far and Psalms 23 sayS in part "THE LORD IS MY SHEPPARD I SHALL NOT WANT".

Every one of us need God so therefore we must want him. If you say God you are Lord, my Lord then Psalms 23 must be read accordingly meaning it should be read this way 'THE LORD IS MY SHEPPARD I DO NEED AND WANT"

"MY GOD YOU ARE MY LORD AND SHEPPARD I NEED AND WANT YOU IN ALL THAT I DO.

"GOD YOU ARE MY SHEPPARD I NEED AND WANT YOU THIS MORNING BECAUSE I CANNOT GO ON WITHOUT YOU. PLEASE GOD MAKE ME TO LIE DOWN IN YOUR GREEN PASTURES AND RESTORE MY SOUL. YEA THOUGH I WALK IN THE SHADOW OF DEATH I WILL FEAR NO EVIL BECAUSE YOU ARE MY ROD AND MY STAFF AND YOU DO COMFORT ME. GOD YOU ARE MY ROCK AND MY SHIELD MY PROTECTOR IN THIS STORM" Pray in this like manner and never tell God that you do not want him because we need him. You can take out the want and just keep the need.

Psalms 1 (one) is the psalms that we must live by and adhere to. Know this psalms and live by it and no evil whether spiritual or physical can touch or harm you. Adhere to Psalms 1 and you will live forever in God's abode. This is why I say and tell you to buy in holy places meaning places that are honest, clean and good. Go to stores and hospitals that uphold the values of God. They must be clean and have the interest of God in their hearts.

Remember God will make it that no evil can come to that hospital. God will only send his people to your hospital, grocery store, hotel you name it God will send his good people there.

If you go out with your friends go to clean clubs. Clubs that are family oriented meaning clubs that do not cater to whoredom.

Dance to your heart's content and know your limit when it comes to drinking.

If the clubs have finger foods eat but never drink to get drunk

If you cannot hold your liquor do not drive home. Never drink and drive take a taxi and stay in a hotel if you know you are going to go overboard with the drinking. Remember others meaning never forget the safety of others. Respect life because the next man wants to live too.

Cherish walking because all of you know how much I truly love to walk but never walk alone because God's angels do not walk alone.

Do not indulge in walking the streets late at nights because the wicked loveth the darkness of the night. Teach your children this as well.

Remember evil walk day and night but they loveth the night even more.

Know the woman you lay with because like I said some are Delilah's and yes some men are Delilah's too.

Do not practice your children nor yourself to go to the churches, mosques, shrines or synagogues of the wicked because God does not reside in any of them.

Never forget that no one can convert you to God because God is the truth within you. God is not a religion and no man on the face of this planet can educate you on God accept God himself. If he has ordained you to write a book write the book based on the truth God has given you and not on the truth of what man has given you.

Know this God will infinitely never ever use the books of man to educate you about him because God is not man he is energy but he can show you himself in the form or way that you can see and comprehend him.

Remember to teach your children right and raise them in truth. Truly love them and not just love them.

Never do as the heathens do by saying you are going to adopt a child this is a sin. If a mother cannot raise her child and say can you take my child and look after him or her and you can do so do it but the mother that has given you that child cannot ask for that child in return. You are responsible for that child so raise that child as one of your own in the truth and true love of God.

Remember you can bend a tree to walk in the good ways of God from he or she is young but when that tree gets older it is harder to bend.

Do not follow people and say my ancestors were enslaved. Yes they were but we have forgotten that our own did sell us out and mothers and fathers are doing this today. It is called human trafficking.

Remember never pick up the fight of another man because you do not know what he or she is fighting about. Leave them alone because you will never know the truth of what they are fighting about.

If they ask for your advice and you have none to give give none and refer to God.

Remember the heathens tell you to have dominion and control but do not follow them because God controls or dominate no one.

The heathens will tell you you must do this this and this to get to God follow them not. Walk away because God tells no one to follow or worship him. We all have a choice and the choice that we make is binding and God cannot go against it. Humanity makes choices and a lot of times those choices are bad so we have to face the consequences.

Let no man tell you to veil your wife and your children. This is an abomination of sin as well as an abomination unto God because no child cometh into this world veiled meaning wearing a face veil. Yes I have heard stories of children born with a veil over their face but I have never seen it nor has God educated me on this so therefore I will not comment on it. I would assume this has to do with the placenta at birth but like I said I have not seen this I have only heard of this.

Remember God has nothing to hide and neither should man.

Know that none of the brides or the children of heaven wears a face veil. This I have seen so no man can dispute it. Not even the lady that sits around the crystal city wears a face veil so do not practice this or conform to this because it is wrong and yes it is sinful and an abomination unto God. Wearing face veils is the Babylonian way because they need to hide their shame of the disgraceful and unlawful acts that they commit and one of those acts are intermarrying with members of their own family. This was done with Abraham because he did practice incest – meaning he married his own – his own half sister and this is unlawful and wrong in the eyes of God and man. If anyone say it is not so refer them to their own bibles the one they hold in high esteem.

Never be like the heathens because they tell you and force their wrongs upon you and say it is the law when they know otherwise.

Never have more than one wife at the same time this is unlawful and a grave sin because God never gave man permission to marry more than one wife.

Have one lifetime partner and never go outside your marriage to fulfill your sexual desires this is adultery and a sin and God will hate you for this.

Divorce are provided for by God but know and do this if you have ended your relationship with someone go before God and man and let them divorce you from their record. Many of us divorce by man's standard but none divorce by God's. Once both parties have dissolved the marriage go to God and dissolve it also because according to God's records you are still married if you do not come to him for a divorce and this is adultery.

If you are in a committed relationship go before God and dissolve the union because in God's eyes you are married to that person and that union is still in his record books.

Let not the heathen tell you if you kill you will get to paradise. This is infinitely wrong and sinful the only paradise you will see is the paradise of hell. You will see Satan and his pack of demons. Know that no one can kill for God because God is life and not death. Death kills not God.

Never kill or take up arms for the death or any dead prophets because those that you think are in heaven they reside in hell with the devil – Satan.

Know this because I am telling you this. God do not send prophets he send messengers to deliver his message and if God chose you you are well chosen.

Many things you will not understand because you will see death before you. You will know when people are going to die. You will see faces infront of you and yes the dead will come to you. Never listen to the heathens and say this cannot happen you are delusional because you are not God is showing you things that they cannot see.

A Babylonian asked me this if I see things before me and I denied it. Not because I feared for myself but because she was a Babylonian working as a psychologist and you know they way some of these people are. They will evaluate you as psychotic and deranged. Know infinitely know that your culture is not their culture and the truth that God gives you they will kill you for it and yes they will turn society against you because they have not the truth.

Know that many black people can see the dead face to face. Don't believe in spooks because the dead are humans meaning they have human characteristics. I am sorry if I explained this and it confused you.

Let's try it this way. As you see yourself you will see the dead.

Know that God does not use fire evil does. There is something called a rolling calf and this is why some people worship the cow and make graven images of the cow. A rolling calf is a cow that comes in the form of a ball of fire. It is pure evil because it is sent to kill you. You see these beast late at night trust me you do not want to be around when they are around. Stay in your home they are that dangerous.

Let no one tell you that the dead does not call you because some do and you can hear them call your name so be careful how you answer because the lot of them are evil and they will take your life because some do come to kill you.

Know who you eat from because some people say they are with you but they are against you.

Know that wicked and evil people use food to catch you so please do not eat from unclean people.

Trust me some of our own Jamaican's are nasty and filthy. Trust me some look good but the heart is worse than sin it is that vile. Trust me some of the women do use their period – blood for evil to tie you. If you hear a Jamaican man tell you they do not eat or drink red peas soup from a woman when they are on their period do not laugh they know what they are talking about.

Remember I told you about the meat of swine – pork well some people use this to tie you meaning write your name on parchment paper and tie you. Keep you down.

Some have your name on parchment paper and walk on it to keep you down.

Some will give you things in your drinks to enlarge your belly and no matter how much you go to the doctor the doctor will never find what ails you so be careful of evil and wicked people.

Don't think that they won't sprinkle powder at your door for you to step over it they will.

They will plant things at your gate to kill you so put nothing past evil.

Do not listen to people and say if you are of God this will not happen to you. Trust me it will because you are associated with evil meaning you have evil around you so evil is capable of anything.

Do not practice yourself or your children to wear the clothes of others because many use your clothing for evil.

If you are giving away your clothes know who to give it to because your heart may be clean but the other person's heart is filthy.

Remember people do for a place in hell and none do for a place with God in his abode.

Never ever forget that evil lies and it is very cunning – deceitful so seek favour in all that you do from God if you are not sure.

Always be there for your children and let no woman tell you you spend too much time with your children. They are yours so do right by them.

If anyone asks can your children get you into heaven meaning God's abode tell them infinitely no. No one can get you into God's abode apart from you.

It is not a sin to not have children. It is better to have none than be like the heathens that have 18 – 20 and cannot feed them or raise them right.

If you want only 2 children have only two. Have two not one because one is lonely.

If you want four have four but make sure you can provide for them the right and proper way and remember ask God before hand to take the genes of sin from your children. Ask God for good clean and obedient children. Our forefathers forgot to do this and if you read the book of lies – meaning the book of death which is the bible it tells you how the children of Israel and Judah walked in the ways of sin and evil. How they did abominable acts before God.

Yes humanity is still doing it today hence I will tell you there are many mansions in hell but very few in God's abode.

Many will tell you about Jesus but run meaning do not listen because I told you Jesus does not exist the story is of the devil meaning mother and child. This child is the first daughter of sin and the Roman

Catholic Church uphold this sinful lie until this day.

Satan has three (3) daughters and each have a six on their forehead. This is their mark because this is how it was shown to me. The six for each child is lying down.

6+6+6 = 18 add another 6 = 24 meaning the devil has 24000 to reign hence we have the 24 hour clock and the 24 hour day.

3 daughters each have 6 and you have to include Satan to make 24. Do not add Eve the mother of Sin because evil is female in the physical and spiritual world. Evil cannot change hence the two (2) XX's. This does not mean all women are evil. If you say all women are evil you would be wrong because I told you God is female in the physical and male in the spiritual and if you ask God to show you him and comfort you he will show you him as a female, a open door, a voice in the cloud this is why I tell you to know what God is trying to tell you.

Make it your point and duty to be in your home before dusk – before it gets dark. I know because of work schedules this will be hard but try or chose your hours wisely. If you do not have a reason to be on the streets at nights go home. Be in the comforts of your home. Trust me there are many things you can do at home and yes this includes doing some house work but not all the time.

Make nighttime family time by helping your kids with their homework

Play video games

Listen to your children's music

Play board games

Make them a homemade treat

Just make nighttime family time and enjoy your family.

Many things I repeated but I cannot help it. Take heed to good council and do not walk in the ways of sin or you will die. You will regret it. Make God apart of your good life and live.

Mother

My children the gift of love is embedded within each and every one of you

You are hope, true love, children of a brighter tomorrow

You are children of God

Children of Love – true love

My children, great is my love for you

I love you all unconditionally.

So this book I dedicate to you, all four of you. Read each word and humble yourself unto them. God will teach you all and give you knowledge.

All you have to do is wait on him, be patient.

My children, love is the key, it is the key to God's heart, the key to residing with him in paradise. When you truly love him you are on your way to becoming clean.

I love you all

Love always and forever

Mother

Other books by Michelle Jean

Behind the Scars

My Collective A Collection of Prayers Sayings and Poems

My Collective the Other Side of Me

Blackman Redemption

Blackman Redemption – The Rise and Fall of Jamaica

Blackman Redemption – The Truth about God

Ode to Mr. Dean Fraser

A Little Talk/A Time For Fun and Play

Prayers

Love Bound

Love Bound Book Two

Saving America From a Woman's Perspective